LAW
ENFORCEMENT
AND COMMUNITY
RELATIONS

LAW ENFORCEMENT AND COMMUNITY RELATIONS

RICHARD E. FARMER

Cape Cod Community College

VICTOR A. KOWALEWSKI

University of Wisconsin at Platteville

52753

RESTON PUBLISHING COMPANY, INC.
Reston, Virginia

A Prentice-Hall Company

Library of Congress Cataloging in Publication Data

Farmer, Richard E
    Law enforcement and community relations.

    Bibliography: p. 159
    Includes index.
    1. Public relations—Police.　2. Police social
work.　3. Crisis intervention (Psychiatry)
I. Kowalewski, Victor A.,　joint author.
II. Title.
HV7936.P8F37　　　　659.2′9′363.2　　　　75-43526
ISBN 0-87909-434-6

© 1976 by
Reston Publishing Company, Inc.
A Prentice-Hall Company
Reston, Virginia 22090

10　9　8　7　6　5　4　3　2　1

Printed in the United States of America.

To
Bonnie and **Joyce**
For love, support, and patience (sometimes)

Contents

Preface

Police-community relations programs were created literally by the hundreds in the late 1960s in an effort to overcome a perceived gap between police and other members of the community. In the past few years police administrators and other citizens have sharply questioned the basic concepts behind many police-community relations efforts.

We have looked at some of the functions of existing programs and have suggested a variety of ways in which police agencies may use community relations programs to enhance the activities of the entire department. A basic premise of this book is twofold: First, that the police must accept responsibility for providing a wide variety of non-enforcement functions and secondly, that increasing accountability to the community will be a major public concern in the next decade.

This volume is the product of two authors with often divergent views of police and their role in society. Within this framework of diversity there is a basic agreement about the urgent need for a specific, even ruthless, re-examination of the concept of police-community relations.

In Chapter 1, Victor Kowalewski briefly examines the history of police-community relations and outlines some basic concepts for change.

Chapters 3, 5, 8 and 10 reflect his experience as an urban affairs journalist and as an ombudsman for a medium-sized city, as well as his training and beliefs about police-community relations.

In Chapter 2, Richard Farmer outlines the concept of the full service model for police services. Chapters 4, 6, and 9 reflect his research into methods of change for police administration, and his experience as a line police officer.

We especially wish to thank Dr. Robert Meier, of the University of New Haven, for contributing Chapter 7 in which he shares his special knowledge of psychology, especially in the area of human interaction.

The authors owe a special debt to Joyce Kowalewski for critical comments, encouragement, style editing and for typing this volume. Valuable research help and patience were provided by the staff of the Criminal Justice Reference and Information Center, University of Wisconsin at Madison. Their assistance turned research from a drudgery into a genuine pleasure.

Encouragement was offered by W. Brooks Smith, Division of Human Services, Cape Cod Community College. Thanks are due to Betsy Rock and Martha Votolato for their work in typing and to Cindy Rogness for her assistance.

Support for this project originated from the staff of the Division of Criminal Justice, University of New Haven, directed by L. Craig Parker. We wish to give special thanks to Gerald Robbin for his continuous encouragement and comments during the early stages of preparation and to Kay Allard who facilitated much of the early research for this volume.

RICHARD E. FARMER
VICTOR A. KOWALEWSKI

〔 1 〕

Police–Community Relations: An Overview

The time has come for a reevaluation of the role of police-community relations as part of the activity of law enforcement agencies. The authors suggest that the driving force which led to the creation of community relations units, particularly in larger departments, was a direct reaction, an attempt to "do something," to cope with unrest among youth and the urban poor that marked the close of the 1960s.

This reactive approach to dealing with community relations was never appropriate; for in essence it was an attempt to deal with the public on the basis of fear—fear that "something might happen" if the police did not move to establish better communications with youth and minorities in particular and with the public in general.

• SOME PROPOSALS
FOR PCR

A more appropriate police approach to the problem of developing community relations lies in the following propositions.

1 · Police-community relations are those activities undertaken by a department from a position of strength, confidence and leadership which result in a genuine, continuing dialogue between officers and all citizens.

2 · Police-community relations also involve building strong lines

3

of communication within the department. Line officers, in particular, should develop a positive approach toward providing the varied services the public expects from the police.

The job of a police-community relations officer or unit thus involves development of a program of continual training and consultation within the entire department. This "in house" task is just as vital as opening lines of contact with civilians.

Open Communication • The effective community relations unit will be called upon not only to devise departmental training in what we refer to as the "full service model," but also to provide both counseling and support for officers in helping them cope with the high level of stress to which they are exposed.

In addition, the police need to build open communication with the total community. Programs that are aimed at any one segment of a community such as youth, minorities, or the poor begin under a heavy handicap. For example, there is no question that relations between black and Hispanic citizens and the police need strengthening; yet we contend with equal vigor that relations with minorities and youth are not the sole problem or even the most important issue facing many departments.

Open communication with the total community can only be accomplished through approaches that have some real substance—approaches that create real exchanges of views between police officers and other citizens.

The opportunity for "real exchanges" usually occurs on a one-to-one basis or in small group settings. Police should concentrate their energies on trying to establish contact with the public through this approach.

A number of departments have elected to form special police-community relations units or to assign individual officers the task of developing police-community relations by means of public relations efforts and community service projects. The officer or unit may also have the task of representing the department in dealings with local social service agencies.

Appropriate PCR Tasks • The various tasks usually assigned to PCR officers or units need further examination. At this time, a few preliminary comments seem in order.

First of all, a clear distinction should be made between the development of meaningful communication with the public and routine public relations activities. Public relations is a legitimate part of the work of a community relations unit when department policies, programs, or standards are explained to the public either through the media or by personal appearances at civic functions, school meetings and so on.

However, when unit personnel or other department members spend an inordinate amount of time carrying out public relations tasks of a rather trite nature, time is being wasted and the image of the department is not enhanced but lowered.

For instance, during one seminar on police-community relations an officer expressed the view that he had been most successful during his work with youth. "I spoke to approximately 14,200 school children last year," he boasted. When asked what opportunity he had for personal contact with the students, he replied, "Well, they wave at me when I drive by."

Again, foundations of continuing communication with the public are not being built when all the public hears of the chief of police (or other high command officer) is the usual statement exhorting against the discharge of fireworks on the fourth of July, or promoting safe driving in winter weather, or a photo depicting the purchase of the first sheet of Easter Seals.

We believe that the public is increasingly looking toward public officials of all ranks for signs of strong leadership and a high level of competence in carrying out their duties. Good public relations involves *all* members of a department, not just the community relations unit—although the latter may spearhead such efforts. It is the line officer who plays an important, perhaps pivotal role in building good public relations.

When officers carry out their duties with an air of confidence and competence and a genuine interest in citizen requests for non-criminal enforcement services, the stage is set for closer citizen-police cooperation toward combatting crime and creating an orderly society.

The Role of the Line Officer • Line officers should be encouraged to take responsibility in personally meeting service requests. Training should be aimed at developing the line officer's skills as a helping agent. Skillful execution of difficult social service situations should be recognized by the department with an appropriate citation. In evaluating a line officer's performance, such accomplishments should carry as much weight in determining promotion as skillful handling of law enforcement incidents.

• IMPLICATIONS OF THE FULL SERVICE MODEL FOR PCR

It is suggested that the community service or "full service model" at once takes into account the actual nature of police work and simultaneously builds desired citizen-police relations. The full service model does not subordinate the law enforcement aspect of police work, but recognizes that the vast bulk of requests for police services involve non-enforcement matters. This concept of police work recognizes such requests, for the most part, as being valid and constituting "real" (worthwhile) police work.

However, many officers, at all levels, find the community or full service concept unacceptable. Reiser (1974) for instance has suggested that many young policemen develop a "John Wayne syndrome . . . a tendency to talk tough, to chronically tense muscles, and to develop a kind of tunnel vision in which people are either 'good' or 'bad' guys." (p. 52)

Furthermore, carrying out non-enforcement service requests is seen by some line officers as engaging in "social work"—an activity that has an effete connotation.

Police community relations units, in fact, have been seen by many as a convenient place for line officers and other department staff members to "refer" or to "dump" social service requests that might well have been handled on the spot. At a recent police-social services conference in a medium sized Eastern city, one community relations officer remarked somewhat bitterly that he and his fellow unit members were tabbed as "baby sitters" by other department members.

The existence of a community relations unit should not be used by administrators as a means of discouraging line officers from establishing informal contact with the public, or providing on the spot non-criminal enforcement assistance.

A review of the operations of the community relations unit of a medium sized city by a private consulting firm (Schwartz, Fichtner, Bick and Associates, 1970) underscores the problem:

> The most severe problems (facing the unit) however, are internal. There is a very definite lack of understanding and support of the division's concept and activities by the vast majority of police department personnel. Many men are very reluctant to change their attitudes toward police work in general and police-community relations in particular. (p. 20)

Thus, the community relations unit that is committed to positive action and community leadership faces two immediate problems. The first task is to convince fellow officers that their unit has a significant role in department operations and involves "real police work." The second is, of course, to help officers at all levels accept the proposition that policing involves handling, in a highly systematic fashion, a wide variety of human concerns that fall outside of criminal enforcement related tasks.

The operation of community relations units will be discussed in greater detail elsewhere in this book. However, at this juncture it is important to restress an earlier proposition: much of the work in promoting sound, consistent community relations policies must take place within the total department and involve a commitment of all officers and administrators.

Perhaps the most difficult aspect of developing the concept of the full service model within a department is that line officers are likely to object to the new demands that they see arising from a total commitment to such a model. Strong, consistent support and follow up must be provided by administrators and police-community relations units to assist officers in dealing with their reservations, in order to develop a viable full service model.

Role Conflict and Change • Much has been written about a certain type of stress known as *role conflict* which tends to inhibit change. It is important to identify this conflict, study the barriers, and move to overcome their effects. Role conflict (for our purposes) is the pull of different expectations for job performance held by training academies, fellow officers, and the public.

Perhaps too much emphasis has been placed on various studies and general attention to the problem of role conflict facing police. Change in any highly structured institution is often accompanied by considerable discomfort for some within those institutions, yet change invariably does take place.

It is time that more stress is placed on the ability of police personnel to change—to experience personal growth. To paraphrase Carkhuff and Berenson (1967), the task facing police administrators and community relations specialists is to identify ways of helping fellow officers to find "nourishment," i.e., satisfaction in their jobs.

The following chapters will examine some of the tools available to officers at both line and staff levels to bring about constructive change and to live comfortably with it. In addition, specific examples are given of simple, direct programs undertaken by several departments to create closer community ties.

All of these program efforts require little in the way of capital expenditure—they were selected as examples for that very reason. What is required for program success by police officers is genuine commitment to the program's ideals and a great amount of consistent, gut level work on the part of the particular law enforcement agency.

(2)

The Full Service Model

The role of the police has come under close examination in recent years. Numerous debates have occurred concerning the role of the police, with both professional practitioners and academics offering their enlightened positions. It is a difficult task to sort through the maze of arguments and definitions to find the appropriate standard. Niederhoffer (1967) writes:

> The policeman is a Rorschach in uniform as he patrols his beat. His occupational accoutrements—shield, nightstick, gun, and summons book —clothe him in a mantle of symbolism that stimulates fantasy and projection. (p. 1)

The police role represents a variety of functions to a variety of individuals. There are those who maintain that the police officer should be a Philosopher, Guide, and Friend (Cumming, Cumming, and Edell, 1965), or that the police officer should be a helper (Kowalewski, 1974). Others strongly maintain that the line officer should be concerned with the preservation of the peace, protection of life and property, enforcement of laws, and detection of law breakers (Garmire, 1968). The enforcement function is also proposed as the *only* function for police, and it is considered they should not be called upon to perform other duties (Lohman & Misner, 1967; National Advisory Commission on Civil Disorders, 1968; President's Commission on Law Enforcement and the Administration of Justice, 1967).

Yet what the role of the police is or should be remains problematic for both the professional practitioner and the law enforcement academic. This chapter will examine the nature of roles and the police and look at the community or full service orientation.

•   ROLE THEORY AND
ROLE CONFLICT

What is a "role" and how does the concept of role theory apply to police organizations and behavior? Generally, a role is a set of patterned behaviors associated with a particular social position (Broom & Selznick, 1970). This definition may be further distinguished by the concepts of ideal and actual roles. The role itself is somewhat analogous to the formal job description governing the prescribed behavior of an individual performing the particular role. The ideal role tells the actor the rights, duties, and expectations of the job he is to perform. The actual role is what the actor does in reality with his role, regardless of the prescribed behavior. The actual role, as distinct from the ideal role, is subject to the particular social setting and the actor's personality. The difference, then, is that the ideal role may be seen as sterile and existing in a vacuum, while the actual role is subject to change and outside pressures. Role performance consists of both the ideal and the actual role. Indeed the ideal role represents a foundation upon which the individual builds his actual role performance.

Concerning police behavior, the existence of both the ideal and actual roles is readily evident. The police recruit learns his ideal role in training at the academy. As the recruit becomes a rookie his actual role takes over as he begins to perform his duties on the street. While at the academy, the new recruit learns his duties as a police officer. He learns the fundamentals and techniques of modern law enforcement. However, this learning takes place in the classroom and is often removed from the particular social setting and the personality of the recruit. When the recruit graduates from the academy, he begins learning his actual role. This learning does not take place by reading and listening to lectures as in the classroom, but by trial and error and by observation of other police officers. Essentiallly, roles are a learned phenomenon. The recruit/rookie learns both types of roles.

Role Conflict: An Example   •   The following scenario illustrates this point: John, a new rookie, has just graduated from the police academy and has been assigned to the motorized patrol division. He and his partner Bill, a twelve year veteran of the force, patrol their sector for about an hour. They then proceed to park their vehicle behind a large shopping center. When John asks Bill what they are doing, Bill informs him that they are going to "sleep" for a while, and not to worry about it because everybody does it. John is confused—at the academy he was taught the value of continuous, aggressive patrol to fight crime.

The academy experience obviously taught John the ideal role for police officers. John is now confronted by one actual role of a particular officer by observing the actions of Bill. Confusion between the ideal and the actual is causing role conflict for John. Role conflict occurs when in the course of role behavior the individual is subjected to conflicting pressures and strains (Broom & Selznick, 1970).

Role conflict is a very common experience for police officers. Constant, conflicting pressures and situations challenge the police officer's role in the society. This conflict may be seen clearly in light of the debate between the service versus the enforcement models of policing. For example, Jack E. Whitehouse (1973) comments:

> The police of yesterday performed a variety of health, welfare and other social service functions. These duties were considered commonplace and essential. There is no indication that there was a problem with what today's social scientists call role conflict. They did not have the advantage of sociologists talking to them about the incompatibility of roles, role conflict, or other trauma. . . . Some modern police officers having had these advantages seem to believe that it is beneath their dignity to perform help type activities. (p. 92)

• PATTERNS OF POLICE FUNCTIONS

In light of the present discussion, what is the function of police in society? What should be the police role? Systems theory and analysis have contributed great insights into the day-to-day functioning of the criminal justice system, and will easily lend itself to the present discussion of the role of the police.

One of the many mandates of the systemic way of approaching problems of organizational behavior or role performance is to look at the actual role functioning rather than to view roles within the context of the stated goals or purposes of the organization. In order to determine what the goals of the police organization should be, it is necessary to look at what the members of the organization do. Traditionally, goals have been viewed as a static element in the organization—any attempt in fact to look at goals within the organization was seen in light of production meeting these stated goals.

> The essential difficulty with this purposive approach is that an organization characteristically includes more or less than is indicated by design. . . . Some of the factors assumed in the design may be lacking or so distorted in operational practice as to be meaningless (Katz & Kahn, 1966, p. 16).

Changing Police Goals • Traditionally, police goals have been concerned with order maintenance, law enforcement, and service. Germann, Day, and Galatti (1962) establish goals for the police as: the prevention of crime and disorder; the preservation of the peace; and the protection of life, property, and individual liberty. Adams (1968) indicates that the police goals are crime prevention and repression, traffic law enforcement, protective patrol services, arbitration in neighborhood and family disputes, apprehension and arrest (or citation or warning) of criminal law violators, and recovery of stolen property.

Law enforcement and order maintenance seem to prevail among the goals for the police. Yet, an examination of the statistics available on what the police actually do indicates that the law enforcement functions of the police occupy relatively few man hours per week. The data in Table 2.1 show the classification of calls to a metropolitan police department.

Analysis of this table indicates that 49.6 percent of calls received by the department are for assistance in personal or interpersonal problems. Another 31.8 percent deal with calls about "things"—such as traffic violations, reports of losses or thefts, calls about unlocked doors, fallen power wires, and so on. Thus, it seems that requests for service occur more frequently than do requests for law enforcement.

James Q. Wilson (1968) reports that in a study of citizen telephone calls to the Syracuse, New York, Police Department only 10.3 percent of the calls could potentially require the police to perform a narrowly defined law enforcement function. Table 2.2 summarizes the findings.

Wilson points out:

> The vast majority of police actions taken in response to citizen calls involve either providing a service (getting a cat out of a tree or taking a person to the hospital) or managing real or alleged conditions of disorder (quarreling families, public drunks, bothersome teen-agers, noisy

Table 2.1   Classification of Calls to the Complaint Desk
             of a Metropolitan Police Department During
             82 Selected Hours in June and July 1961

Type of Call	Number of Calls	Percent of Total
Total	801	100.0
Calls included in analysis	652	81.4
1. Calls about "things"	255	31.8
2. Calls for support	397	49.6
Persistent personal problems	230	28.7
a. Health services	81	10.1
b. Children's problems	83	10.4
c. Incapacitated people	33	4.1
d. Nuisances	33	4.1
Periodic personal problems	167	20.9
a. Disputes	63	7.9
b. Violence	43	5.4
c. Protection	29	3.6
d. Missing persons	11	1.4
e. Youths' behavior	21	2.6
Calls excluded from analysis	149	18.6
Information only	33	4.1
Not police business	28	3.5
Feedback calls	88	11.0

Reprinted from: Elaine Cumming, Ian Cumming, and Laura Edell. Policeman
as Philosopher, Guide and Friend. *Social Problems* 12, 3 (1965), p. 279.

cars, tavern fights). Only a small fraction of these calls involve law
enforcement, such as checking on a prowler, catching a burglar in the
act, or preventing a street robbery. (p. 9)

Further studies support this observation. For instance, out of 394 calls
received by a sector of the Chicago Police Department, 16 percent of
the calls consisted of reported crimes in progress or crimes that had
already occurred; 44 percent consisted of reports of incidents that could
have involved a criminal action (e.g. a disturbance, or an intoxicated
man); and 40 percent consisted of requests for various forms of service
and for information (Rinzel, 1972, p. 61).

Table 2.2   Citizen Complaints Radioed to Patrol Vehicles,
               Syracuse Police Department, June 3-9, 1966
               (based on a one-fifth sample of a week's calls)*

	Calls	Number in Sample	Full Count (Sample Multiplied by 5)	Percent
Information gathering		69	345	22.1
Book and check	2			
Get a report	67			
Service		117	585	37.5
Accidents, illnesses ambulance calls	42			
Animals	8			
Assist a person	1			
Drunk person	8			
Escort vehicle	3			
Fire, power line or tree down	26			
Lost or found person or property	23			
Property damage	6			
Order maintenance		94	470	30.1
Gang disturbance	50			
Family trouble	23			
Assault, fight	9			
Investigation	8			
Neighbor trouble	4			
Law enforcement		32	160	10.3
Burglary in progress	9			
Check a car	5			
Open door, window	8			
Prowler	6			
Make an arrest	4			
Totals		312	1,560	100.0

* Not included are internal calls—that is, those originating with another police
officer (for example, when an officer requests a check on the status of a person
or vehicle or requests the wagon, and so forth)—or purely administrative calls.

Reprinted from: James Q. Wilson. *Varieties of Police Behavior*. Cambridge,
Mass.: Harvard University Press, 1968, p. 18.

Therefore, the evidence suggests that the police spend approximately 80 to 90 percent of their time in service duties. What then does this suggest about the role of the police? The data indicates that it is necessary to establish the service model for the police role. Yet, as Goldstein (1968) has pointed out—despite the distribution of activity, police agents are geared primarily to fight crime. Goldstein further comments:

> This is reflected in all aspects of their operations—in recruitment standards, in the content of training programs, in the operating procedures, and, perhaps most importantly, in the firm set of values and the rather narrow orientation which police generally bring to the handling of those noncriminal matters that are included in the broad range of police functions. "Real" police work is viewed by police officers as the investigation of criminal activity and the identification and apprehension of offenders. (p. 418)

Echoing this same point, James F. Ahern, former chief of the New Haven, Connecticut, Police Department, in testimony before the Joint Economic Committee of Congress states: "I think planning for police is fraud—I mean training for police is a fraud. I do not know of any department that has one (training program) that is really relevant to what a policeman does." (p. 61)

• THE FULL SERVICE MODEL

Given the present role conflict between the enforcement function and the service orientation of the police, what then should be the role of police? In view of the available statistics and studies on the matter of police functions, primary emphasis should be placed on the full service model. This is *not* to suggest that the police should abandon their enforcement functions. To the contrary, the police should certainly retain their duties as enforcers of the law. What is suggested is that the primary orientation and/or model of operation should be aimed at the delivery of services to the community.

What does the community service approach entail? Fink and Sealy (1974), addressing themselves to a new approach for the police, comment:

> The task of the policeman, which has always been difficult, is today almost impossible. Nevertheless, it is clear that any attempt to provide police services to the community must be predicated on an understanding of the community's need for such services, the ability of the organi-

zation to provide such services, and the community's acceptance of the nature, quality, and intention of such services offered.

Given the social realities of the day, the tool that gives the most effective police service is not traditional law enforcement; it may be conflict management—the treatment of disruptive actions to solve problems for the concerned individuals, groups, and sub-communities. To a large extent, successful conflict management depends on the capacity to relate to underlying causes or latent motivations that produce unusual, deviant, or antisocial behavior. (pp. xii-xiii)

Table 2.3 lists the roles for the policeman as a conflict manager.

Table 2.3   The Policeman as a Conflict Manager: Police Roles

Order Maintenance	Community Service	Law Enforcement
Keeping the peace	Health services	Warn and admonish
Regulation of conduct	Referrals to public and private agencies	Issue summons
Crime prevention	Civil law services	Make arrests
Settling disputes	Redress of grievances	
Crisis intervention	Emergency services	

Reprinted from: Joseph Fink & Lloyd G. Sealy. *The Community and the Police —Conflict or Cooperation?* New York: Wiley, 1974, p. xiii, © 1974, Joseph Fink & Lloyd G. Sealy. Reprinted by permission of John Wiley & Sons, Inc.

Thus, the new orientation may be seen as conflict management on the part of the police. The key element, it seems, to Fink and Sealy's argument is the understanding of human behavior. Grange (1974) contends that understanding and knowledge are the best tools for effective police work. Further commenting, E. Wilson Purdy (1966) asserts that: "Understanding, through education, must come to the police family, if we are to fulfill that important position of 'community leader' fully prepared to lead society through today's social upheaval into a better community of tomorrow." (p. 5)

C. Donald Engle (1974) reports a study of police officers' assessments of police training programs. Officers were asked to list and rank in order of importance those aspects of police training which should require more attention in future training programs. Their recommendations are as follows:

1 · Public and/or community relations
2 · Handling emotionally charged situations
3 · Abnormal psychology (recognition of mental disorders)
4 · Human behavior—how it works
5 · Police problems (minority race problems and/or local problems)
6 · Sociology
7 · More experienced police officer instruction
8 · Leadership training
9 · Politics
10 · Drug training
11 · Report writing
12 · State penal code
13 · Chain of evidence
14 · Moral problems of men and women (p. 63)

Engle comments:

> Only four of these areas—report writing, state penal code, chain of evidence, and leadership training might fall within a more narrowly defined police training program. All of the others (with the possible exception of "more experienced police officer instruction") seem to indicate that this group of in-service officer trainees recognize the complexity of their role demands. (p. 63)

The full service model, then, suggests several changes in the role concept of the police. The first change is direct—that of moving from the enforcement orientation to the service level of operations. The second change suggests that in order for the police to move to the service model, understanding through education is necessary. This viewpoint represents a more subtle change in role performance for the police. And this second change may be linked directly to the idea of professionalism for the police.

Professionalism · Garbor and Low (1973) suggest that professionalism for the police exists on two levels—the individual and the departmental. We shall be concerned primarily with professionalism of the individual officer.

Louis Radelet (1966), one of the pioneers in the area of professionalized police, has stated that personal professionalism is a balance between the benefits accruing to the police—especially higher pay, greater respect, and public support—and a new set of obligations. Developing higher standards of education and a professional attitude are the foremost of these obligations.

Higher education is the *sine qua non* for developing a professionalized police, in the sense that higher education will help the police in understanding human behavior. Albert Reiss (1969) cogently stated the idea of the professional attitude:

> I mean by professionalization that the police are trained and highly trained to remove themselves from involvement in situations. This does not necessarily mean that one changes attitudes fundamentally but one teaches them to learn to deal with their attitudes in situations (of stress). In short, one has to create a kind of collegial order in which the responsibility is to one's duty and what one does rather than to one's self. (p. 52)

Thus, professionalization can be viewed as a key element in the construction of the full service approach. Recapitulating briefly, then, we can see that the role of the police has been traditionally that of law enforcement. Recent statistics and studies have indicated that a role change is necessary for the police. As pointed out earlier, estimates of time spent performing enforcement functions vary between 10 and 20 percent of the workload. The remaining 80 to 90 percent of the police function deals with social/community service duties. The community service orientation therefore has been offered as a solution to the disparity. The basic philosophy of the full service argument revolves around what the police actually do. Why should police training and primary operational emphasis be geared for that portion of police duties that occupies a relatively small amount of hours per day? It is thus proposed that the police role should be that of service, coupled with a lesser emphasis on the enforcement function.

Several methods of service have been proposed for the police. Kowalewski (1974) views the police role as that of helper. According to his concept, modelled after the philosophy of the radical school, policemen are considered as professional helpers in much the same light as are psychiatrists, psychologists, and social workers. The radical school has attempted to redefine the concept of professionalism. The radical concept of the police role suggests that the police officer is in a unique position within the community in regard to services performed, and that he has both the capacity and the skills necessary to perform a vital helping role in the community. Yet, the line police officer is often caught up in the controversy over professionalism. To some members of traditional helping agencies, the policeman is "not professional enough to be entrusted with carrying out tasks that one would assign to the rawest intake worker" (p. 7). However, to the general public the line officer must be and should be available to carry out a variety of helping oriented duties with an air of competence and confidence.

Presently, helping tasks are often referred to a community relations unit which, instead of defining the police role to the general public, ends up being a departmental social service bureau. This unit performs a vast range of social services, many of which could be carried out by line officers if they had the desire to act and a sense of confidence in their own ability to deal with such a situation.

Paving the Way for Community Service • Martin Reiser (1967) proposes that the police be viewed as mental health agents:

> The policeman has long occupied a unique role in the mental health resources in the community, although the significance of this function has not always been fully understood or appreciated. As the omnipresent, primary community agent in human services, he is forced to deal with a wide spectrum of human problems and behavioral crises. There are approximately 400,000 policemen, but because he is the only community agent available seven days a week around the clock the modern police professional is obligated to increase his behavioral science expertise and accept the legitimacy of his role as mental health agent. (p. 1)

Reiser states that much police activity includes intervening in family disputes, handling mentally disturbed and suicidal individuals, dealing with rape and child abuse victims, and locating lost or runaway children and senile citizens. In order to deal effectively with these situations, the police officer must be specially trained and educated in the field of behavioral science. The concepts of *crisis intervention* and *crisis management* should occupy a key position in this training. Early recognition, intervention, counseling, and referral techniques should be given a primary status position at the police academy training center.

In essence, Reiser states that the police officer has to become a social scientist. The officer must realize that he is dealing primarily with human problems and so must become a specialist in human relations if he is to be effective. Reiser further comments:

> In the foreseeable future, the police will continue to play an important role in the front-line of the mental health system. Much like a triage team, they will be called upon to intervene, evaluate, and "diagnose," provide brief crisis counseling, and refer for more intensive help. (p. 1)

Cumming, Cumming, and Edell (1965) view the police officer as the individual who must supply support to persons with personal or interpersonal problems. The police officer accomplishes this support either by friendly sympathy, by feeding authoritative information into the troubled situation, or by helping to develop a resolution. Studies that these authors have undertaken show that the police officer spends approximately 50 percent of his time in supportive actions. They indicate three reasons for this:

> First, the policeman has to do much of what he does because he is on duty at times of the day when no other agent is available. Second, he deals with the problems of a group of people—the poor and the ignorant —that studies of our own and others have shown no other agent to be anxious to serve and, third, the knowledge of, and access to, very few other agents. (p. 278)

Thus, the policeman is required to perform certain social service functions to the community because he is available and perhaps because no one else will provide the same services.

The authors strongly suggest that the full service model is fundamental to the police role in society. In view of what police do, it is necessary for the police to reconsider present role definitions. Since community service is what the police spend most of their time doing, it would seem logical for the police to adopt the service model as the basis of their organizational behavior.

This has significant implications for present methods of police organizational functioning. During the social unrest of the 1960s, many police departments attempted to deal with the inner city tensions by the creation of the police-community relations unit. The President's Commission on Law Enforcement and the Administration of Justice (1967) even proposed that the police create the position of Community Service Officer (CSO) in order to cope with the problems. Traditionally, the PCR unit was responsible for any community service functions that the police were required to perform. The line police officer was left to enforce the laws on his beat, and the so-called social workers in the PCR unit were left to do the "unimportant" duties.

It is suggested that all police officers should become, in effect, mini police-community relations units—the police officer should become the social worker, the psychiatrist, the priest, the guide, and the friend. It is *not* suggested that the police abolish the enforcement function. Rather, the enforcement and the service function should go hand in hand. Policemen, because they are the visible, direct arm of the government and the rule of law must certainly maintain their enforcement duties. However, the police must adopt as their primary goal a service orientation. The policeman should act as an Ombudsman in behalf of the community and the government.

On the one hand, the police should perform certain vital functions or services to the community. Included in these services are the enforcement of the laws and the apprehension of law breakers. On the other hand, the police must act in behalf of the duly recognized government in maintaining order within the society. These are not necessarily antithetical duties. Services to the community, of which law enforcement and order maintenance are an inextricable part, are the police function. Law enforcement and order maintenance then, are actually social services to the community and should be viewed as such.

Given the complex, multi-problem nature of man in today's society, the police have to deal with a large number of conflicting situations. Effective policing requires more than mere enforcement and maintenance of order. Effective policing requires a certain sensitivity, a sense of professionalism, in order to cope with the maze of problems in society. The 24 hour availability of the police means that officers will continue to be the initial representatives of the community to be called upon to deal with such wide ranging multi-problems as family disputes, mental and physical illnesses, missing persons, drug abuse, crime, youth problems, and other such concerns. It is time to lay to rest the myth that "real" police work is law enforcement, the high speed chase, shoot-outs with bank robbers, or riot control. Certainly these are a part of policing, but they do not constitute the total role concept.

Finally, it is time to discount still another myth surrounding the police. The police as a group *are* equipped to deal with many types of social service problems, contrary to what some may believe. There is a growing body of evidence which suggests that with proper training, police officers can be highly effective in certain social situations, particularly crisis intervention problems such as family disputes.

3

Social Services
and
Police-Community
Relations

It has been shown that the vast bulk of requests made to police for various services are of a social service or order maintenance nature and do not involve criminal enforcement tasks.

There is every indication that social service demands on local police and other enforcement agencies will increase, not decrease, during the next decade. This must be accepted as a fact by law enforcement administrators, particularly those who see police work in traditional terms—namely that the bulk of the department's activities or concerns should be related to the enforcement of various state and local statutes concerning crime-related activity.

In the full service model law enforcement, order maintenance and provision for social service functions are all valid concerns of local law enforcement agencies. It has also been contended that these agencies and their personnel are well equipped to provide such social services to the community.

Yet, while the public demands provision of social services, it also expects that police and other enforcement bodies will move vigorously against a perceived rapid increase in criminal activity. Clearly this poses a dilemma for the police administrator who is asked to be responsive to what must seem at times an incompatible, growing list of service requests.

There are two possible solutions to the problem of dealing with nonenforcement service requests. Department administrators may take the stance that such requests are no longer the proper concern of police departments. They may well point to the rapid growth of a myriad of private and public agencies since the 1930s whose sole purpose is to provide social services. The response of these administrators might well be that contact between police and these service agencies should be limited to the automatic referral of nearly all nonenforcement requests to these groups for action.

But as the National Advisory Commission on Criminal Justice Standards and Goals (1973) observed in discussing the handling of intoxicated individuals, "the twenty four hour availability and jurisdictional wide deployment of police officers will undoubtedly cause local governments to rely upon them to locate and take into custody acutely intoxicated persons." (p. 108) The commission has rightly pointed up two key factors which make police departments particularly appropriate as deliverers of social services—namely, 24 hour availability, and the authority to act for the community in dealing with a wide range of concerns.

Local law enforcement agencies therefore have means to intervene positively in many social service-order maintenance situations (such as domestic disputes) that are not available to other community helping agencies.

Furthermore, the role of the line police officer as a helping agent is becoming increasingly recognized by a variety of sources. Martin Reiser, psychologist, Los Angeles Police Department, has increasingly stressed the role of the line officer as a mental health agent (1972, 1974).

Therefore there is no valid reason, either from the point of view of the public interest or law enforcement agency priorities for police administrators to take the stance that social service requests are a minor or inappropriate concern of local police departments.

• PLANNING FOR COMMUNITY SERVICE

The affirmative option for administrators is to establish systematic working relationships with community groups and individuals to identify social service requests. This should be followed up by establishing permanent, positive ties with other social service delivery agencies in the community to plan how to deliver services.

A note of caution: while law enforcement agencies should be receptive to service requests, the department should not undertake service tasks that cannot be fulfilled in a professional manner. Simply put, the department that ignores community social service needs is in trouble.

So is the department that goes to the other extreme and tries to be all things to all people.

Final responsibility for such decisions still lies with the commanding officer. He should make his decision on provision of services in clear, unmistakable terms to the community.

The type of working relationship we propose at once recognizes police responsibilities for the provision of a wide range of social services yet also suggests that it is vital that other social service agencies carry out their responsibilities in meeting community demands. Most likely, the public really does not care who provides these services as long as they are delivered in a systematic, orderly fashion.

Therefore it is essential that police and other helping professionals begin to work toward a cooperative effort that will conserve the time, monies, and energies of all concerned and yet also carry out the public business in a systematic fashion.

In this chapter we will examine the experience of two Eastern communities, Newbarrow and Manford, in their attempts to establish effective liaison between police and other helping agencies. This approach will be contrasted with the recently initiated Community Control Project of San Diego, California. The methods employed by these cities of different size are particularly applicable to a wide variety of communities throughout the country—primarily because they offer examples of innovative attempts to bring the police closer to their clients, and at the same time enhance their ability to work effectively with other helping agencies.

• THE NEWBARROW EXPERIENCE

In Newbarrow, administrators of that city's 164 man police department found themselves confronted with a rapidly growing demand for a variety of nonenforcement social services. From 1970 to 1973 service requests, both for law enforcement and nonenforcement tasks rose from 20,733 to an estimated 30,000-plus in 1973. Allowing for increased police efficiency in record keeping, the volume of requests in real terms was substantial, considering that the population of the city remained nearly constant during this period.

Two factors in particular were most likely responsible for the new service requests: the introduction of a universal 911 emergency telephone system, and a sharp rise in citizen expectations concerning the availability of police services at the local level.

The department police-community relations unit, along with its police planner were particularly concerned about the department's capacity to handle the increasing flow of service requests. It had been a standing policy of the Newbarrow Police that all requests should receive some form of direct response from the department.

While this was an admirable service goal, it placed a heavy responsibility on those receiving 911 calls to make quick, precise judgments about the type of action to take in meeting the problem.

The PCR unit took the stance that since an estimated 70% of these requests involved provision of noncriminal enforcement services, the city's public and private social service agencies should be asked to relieve the police of dealing with some of these problems, or at the very least to take part in a cooperative effort toward providing combined resources to bring about speedy systematic provision of services.

In late 1972 the community relations unit and the police planner joined together to sponsor a series of planning sessions that would lead to a city-wide social services conference on improvement of services.

Emphasis was placed on identifying and inviting representatives of various community groups to a series of pre-planning meetings. These sessions, which occupied several weeks, attempted to identify major community social service problems which needed closer examination through conference workshop sessions. The state office of the National Conference of Christians and Jews acted as a resource group in helping the planning committee identify issues. This role was maintained throughout the conference sessions.

The Newbarrow pre-planning sessions reflected the later meetings due to the free and frank discussion and, at times, heated disagreement, not only over the subject matter to be discussed by the total conference, but also over the right of certain groups to serve as spokesmen for particular community interests.

Out of this series of discussions, it was agreed to hold a series of five day-long workshops to consider problems dealing with the following: handling of emergency transportation cases; handling of intoxicated and mentally disturbed patients; handling of lost or missing persons; enforcement of public health and safety codes; and dealing with multiple problem families.

The day-long sessions were structured so that the keynote for a particular day was presented by an expert from the state criminal justice or social service system. Following this, participants adjourned to their workshop sessions for a day-long discussion of one of the chosen topics.

It is suggested that two factors led to often highly useful discussions:

1 · Each workshop was chaired by a moderator who had particular skills or background concerning the topic under discussion. Moreover, an attempt was made to secure workshop
leaders who had specific experience in working through the
group process.

2 · Participants were not allowed to float from one workshop to
another. Panel members were expected to spend all five
sessions working with their fellow panelists in focusing their
full attention on the specific problem at hand.

Components for Conference Success • Perhaps the most important
component in making such a community conference a success is the willingness of panel participants to react fully and freely with each other.
The five day workshop format was particularly successful because it gave
members a chance to deal with each other on a level other than the
cursory, impersonal level on which they normally function.

While not all individual sessions resulted in this type of open exchange, in most cases barriers to communication were removed. Many
participants were able to articulate why they found it difficult to work
with a particular agency, or group of individuals within that agency.

Of equal importance was that attention was focused on a long
standing myth: that the police were being asked to undertake tasks that
they had not generally performed in the past; that they were not capable
of performing these duties, and that other agencies or individuals should
assume these social service responsibilities. An excellent example of this
reevaluation concerned the emergency transportation of individuals to
local hospitals by the police. Police officials had approached the conference with the idea of seeking some means to rid themselves of this
increasingly burdensome responsibility. However, discussions with community service and civic leaders disclosed that the emergency transportation service was highly regarded by the community, which felt that
the police were providing a particularly valuable service in a skillful
manner.

Numerous instances were cited where the police emergency squad
had performed these duties under unusual and difficult circumstances.
In short, the emergency transportation service was seen by both police
and community as something that was not just busy work for the police
but a social service which provided a needed community helping function and enhanced the status of the department. As a result of conference
deliberations, Newbarrow police decided that they would carefully
screen service requests so that only genuine emergency situations would
be met. At the same time, the department upgraded its emergency ve-

hicles and provided additional training for officers assigned to that duty.

However, conferrees agreed that there were certain tasks that police officers should not be asked to carry out. For instance, it had been the established practice for police to act as the enforcing agents for the city's minimum housing code concerning lack of adequate heat. Simply put, this meant that officers equipped with a thermometer were expected to respond to individual complaints from tenants concerning the alleged failure of landlords to maintain heat at a reasonable level.

The task of responding to these complaints, particularly during peak heating months, had become burdensome for the department. As a result of the conference it was agreed that it was more appropriate for the city health department to handle all such complaints regarding inadequate heat, and furthermore that health officials should be responsible for processing all complaints concerning vermin and other health hazards.

Not all conference recommendations have been followed through with the same level of vigor. A continuing municipal problem is the question of how to deal with intoxicated individuals. A key conference recommendation called for a coordinated effort between police, mental health and other allied agencies to bring about a uniform policy for handling such cases. While a number of follow-up meetings have been held, no definitive, systematic working policy has yet been established. Increasing pressure is developing to produce such an effort as the state moves to decriminalize simple public intoxication.

Problems With Professionalization • With this issue, as with many others, one of the major stumbling blocks to cooperation between police and social work personnel is the issue of professionalism. In general, social service staffers tend to view the police as natural adversaries of their clients. The policeman is often perceived as having a narrow, enforcement-oriented, often insensitive perception of community problems. Perhaps most important, the line officer in particular is sometimes seen as being unskilled and ill equipped by either training or temperament to deal sensitively with problems, particularly those labeled crisis intervention situations. Some police, on the other hand, are seen to be defensive with a tendency to overreact to their lack of formal academic credentials, particularly in dealing with those who label themselves as "professionals."

An incident which did not occur at the Newbarrow session but at a similar meeting illustrates the sense of mutual antagonism. The subject under discussion was how to handle the referral of pre-delinquent youth by police to an appropriate youth service agency. The attitude of the police present was summed up by one officer who remarked, after a series of rather inconclusive comments, "Well, the reason I'm here is to have you people with the degrees tell me what to do." While there was no immediate reply from the agency personnel present, one worker remarked following the session that she had doubts about the ability of the agency to work effectively with the police in resolving the problem. While acknowledging that the officers in question had considerable experience in dealing with youth, she voiced the view that they would be unable to respect the confidentiality of the youth. "Well, you know," she commented, "They (the youth officers) are nice guys, but they're really not professionals."

One of the positive effects of the Newbarrow conference, and of a follow-up session held in February 1974 at a nearby university, was that these attitudes could be expressed by both police and social service personnel on a fairly open basis. If members of traditional helping agencies tend to view police as unprofessional in both their training and manner of carrying out their responsibilities, police express annoyance with a perceived unwillingness of social agencies to share information concerning clients with law enforcement officers. In many instances, youth officers in particular indicated that they were seeking information to help them justify not referring a troubled youth to court officials.

A Community Service Blueprint • Those who attended both the Newbarrow sessions and the university workshop generally agreed on a series of suggestions to improve working relationships between police and helping agency personnel. We would suggest that these concepts have a particular value to all communities where there is a question concerning the availability of monies to improve the delivery of services. The following steps do not require an expenditure of monies but rather the expenditure of time, considerable effort, and good faith on the part of law enforcement leadership and their social service counterparts.

1 · It is vital that police and social service agency personnel meet regularly to plan implementation of new social service programs and to devise means of improving the efficiency of existing efforts. Individuals participating in the planning meetings should have the full authority to act for their agencies.

2 · It is important that line workers, both from police and social agencies, be included in the planning process. This simply means that the expertise of those who perform the day-to-day service tasks should be drawn on in developing programs.

3 · Police agencies should fully inform both new recruits and ex-

isting personnel about the availability of social services in their communities and should instruct all staff in methods to be used in making efficient referrals where appropriate.

4 • Where possible, recruit officers should spend some portion of their training period as interns with a local service agency. Obviously for smaller communities this poses a practical problem. One partial solution, however, might be the use of regional training institutes, particularly in rural areas.

This type of interaction is absolutely vital if police are to re-evaluate their role as providers of helping services.

At the same time, traditional public and private social agencies should be challenged by their communities, including the police, to develop new methods of making their services more readily available to the public. There is nothing sacrosanct about the nine to five, five-day week schedule followed by most helping agencies. In fact, rarely do professionals in other fields have such pleasant hours.

In short, private social service agencies should be expected by their communities to explore new and genuinely creative methods of service delivery. Among these might be: extended hours of service; regular provision of weekend services; and greater agency mobility—that is, getting the caseworker or service provider into the field.

A logical extension of this form of police-social agency planning is reported by Treger, Thomson and Jaeck (1974). A three-year experiment with police and social workers working together in the departments of Wheaton and Niles, Illinois, is reported to have yielded significant results in the following areas: increased respect of police and social workers for one another; more appropriate disposition of police actions in the areas of family and marital problems, mental illness, and nuisance violators.

Not all communities have the means in terms of both dollars and personnel to carry out such combined programs. Nor is there always the will for administrators and staff to put aside professional territorial claims to work together and share responsibility on a day-to-day basis.

Perhaps the greatest strength of the Newbarrow model is that it was not a one-shot deal. It brought people together for a series of conferences where specific goals had to be accomplished. Furthermore, it provided an excellent foundation for continuing relationships between a law enforcement agency and the community. This type of workshop series can be conducted with a minimum of red tape and a maximum of communication.

The Newbarrow model was particularly effective in providing police with direct feedback from community representatives about how their services, both as enforcers and as helping agents, were being received.

This type of community-wide planning offers public administrators who are interested both in enhancing their image and in increasing their effectiveness a sound working means for achieving these goals.

• THE MANFORD EXPERIENCE

An excellent example of police playing a vital proactive role in providing leadership in the development of organization of basic community services can be seen through the experience of the Manford Organization of Social Services.

We provide this example both to illustrate the positive role police can and should have in total community planning, and in order to point out some of the difficulties that must be surmounted in order to bring a plan into implementation.

Manford is a sprawling, suburban city with a wide population spread ranging from a small hard-core of traditional New Englanders to suburbanites. A key feature marking the town's social service delivery system was the inability of helping agencies, including the police, to arrange effective communication between themselves, and more importantly, to provide efficient delivery of services to clients.

The city had organized a social services council but that group, through a combination of apathy and inability of community leaders to agree on priorities, had lapsed into inactivity. At the same time, a variety of individual agencies addressing specific concerns had sprung into existence during the 1960s. These ranged from city-wide drug committees to a municipal department of community development. All these groups and the individuals involved, both public and private, were and are sincerely concerned with providing the 50,000 residents of Manford with a complete variety of human services.

This desire, however, could not overcome the confusion and tug of war between interest groups and agencies about which group if any in the city was to have prime responsibility for comprehensive human services planning and delivery.

In early 1974 the Manford Social Services Planning Committee approached the Criminal Justice Department of a nearby university to serve as a resource for organizing a series of workshop meetings that would lead, it was hoped, to the creation of an active, viable community council which would overcome communications confusion and strengthen existing social service delivery programs.

The selection of criminal justice department personnel who had played similar roles in other such planning sessions and the involvement of key police personnel on the workshop steering committee was an acknowledgment of the important stake that the criminal justice system, particularly the police, have in the development of planning comprehensive human resource programs in any community. Preliminary meetings with a steering committee indicated to one consultant (Victor Kowalewski) that while there was a high degree of individual interest and dedication, community leadership lacked a systematic sense of which community problems deserved priority and that a lack of consensus existed concerning the development of a community council.

Using a format that had been developed in Newbarrow and had proven useful in two other similar communities, the steering committee members and consultant devised a two-day workshop series to deal with the major problems which were perceived to be vital for more effective operation of existing programs.

Individual workshops were held concerning information and referral services, provision of emergency services to individual clients, and development of comprehensive community planning.

The workshop sessions were held in April and May 1974. What resulted was a combination of both success and frustration.

Success was achieved in that executives and line members of individual agencies, including the police, were brought together to identify and analyze systematically day-to-day service delivery problems. Interagency communication, in the fullest sense of the word, was enhanced, particularly in the area of emergency services. Responsibilities and procedures were outlined, clarified, and strengthened.

Community problems such as the lack of availability of psychiatric consulting services were identified, with suggestions to overcome this type of service gap explored. Seen in terms of clarifying roles and updating agency staff about the availability or lack of availability of resources, the two-day workshops may be viewed as a success.

The sessions were also helpful in bringing out and putting on the table the often sharp differences between private agencies and representatives of city government about which group should be entrusted with the decision-making power for planning Manford's present and future human services efforts. This laying the cards on the table must be viewed as a positive result of the workshop. However, the Manford session failed to produce the type of genuine community consensus needed to form a single, viable coordinating agency for that city. The fragmentation of ideas and purpose that existed before the conference essentially remained following more than three months of planning, preparation, and discussions.

It would not be unreasonable to view the months of planning by police and other Manford citizens as being so much wasted time in view of what would appear on the surface to be meager results.

But this type of effort in terms of man-hours expended was particularly valuable from the police perspective for two reasons. Police acted in a community leadership role and at the same time obtained much feedback both from social agency leaders and workers concerning the perceived effectiveness of their services.

We cite the Manford example quite deliberately to illustrate that all police ventures in the role of community leadership and social planning will not automatically be effective, and that police participants in such efforts will experience the same sense of frustration and discouragement that plagues planners in every sector of community social activity.

The willingness to continue to work away at the frustrating, petty, and annoying stumbling blocks is the key, in essence, to authentic police-community working relations. The word "working" is used deliberately. The type of active community relations efforts we have proposed will fail if police administrators assume that style and show are substitutes for genuine commitment.

Possible Pitfalls • In short, there is very little reason for continuing police-community communications unless both community and police leadership individuals are fully committed to this concept. These programs can fail from a police point of view due to two fatal flaws:

1 · Lack of real commitment to citizen planning on the part of an administrator. One of the quickest ways to bring a meeting between police and citizens to a screeching halt is for a police representative to acknowledge that he does not know why he is present but that "the chief told me to be here."

2 · Even if there is support for this type of total community planning from administrators, failure will still occur if it is not recognized as a vital source of potential assistance to police in their everyday activities. Middle management and line officers must see clearly the value of spending time (in some cases not on regular duty hours) in taking part in community planning meetings.

At the Newbarrow conference, one line police officer who had been particularly skeptical of the value of such a series of meetings emerged from the conference sessions with an enthusiastic view of what could be accomplished between city police and private social agencies. "Why he's talking like one of us," declared one amazed social worker.

• THE SAN DIEGO EXPERIENCE

For many police administrators the problem of dealing with other social agencies and the community is to bring the concept of PCR from the drawing board and incorporate it into functioning police practice. The San Diego police have recently initiated a patrol development program (the Community Profile Project) aimed at upgrading the performance of the line officer, particularly in relation to his dealings with the community. The program consists of three basic components. First, systematically training the officer to learn his beat; second, encouraging the officer to identify and document the full range of beat problems; and finally, aiding the officer to develop patrol strategies to solve these problems at his level (San Diego Police Department, 1974, p. 1). The first step of the San Diego project is to require each officer to develop "a disciplined and methodical approach to beat knowledge." (p. 4) Officers receive instructions in methods of patrol planning, field observation, data collection, and problem analysis. The aim of developing this "community profile" is to provide the officer with a "reasoned basis on which to develop responsive and innovative patrol goals and strategies in policing his areas of responsibility." (p. 4)

A second major component of the San Diego experiment is that the officer's *beat knowledge* should include an awareness of community structures, such as socio-economic conditions, community leaders, institutions, agencies, and groups, as well as the traditional emphasis on awareness of trends of criminal, noncriminal, traffic, and police-community problems" (p. 4).

Perhaps one of the more interesting approaches of the San Diego project is that officers maintain regular logs of their work which include a range "from ecological studies of their beats to comprehensive analyses of beat problems." (p. 5) These are submitted on a bi-weekly basis to sergeants and then to higher command officers for discussion with the officer of particular concerns occurring in his patrol area. This log-keeping process also provides a tool in assessing the strengths and weaknesses of individual officer performance.

Another major dimension, and perhaps the key to the San Diego experiment is the concept of *beat accountability*. This refers basically to a patrol officer's continuing development of a personal sense of responsibility for the people and problems of his beat. It is manifested by an officer's actual responsiveness to beat conditions, and by his increasing willingness to get involved in the community and to help people solve such problems as pertain to the police service function. (pp. 5-6)

According to the San Diego plan, "community involvement, in this sense, entails a demanding process of police-community interaction oriented to problem-solving, rather than an image-selling program of 'public relations.'" (p. 6) It is important to note that in the concept being practiced in the San Diego program, police-community relations is seen in terms of a *demanding* task which requires a consistent follow-up by the line officer on problems encountered.

For Chief R. L. Hoobler, the project has several important facets. It is an attempt to use a variety of techniques to develop or enhance the role of the line officer—an attempt to return to the concept of the police generalist. The project is also an attempt to develop "goal oriented patrol efforts" rather than patrol activity which is undertaken without any frame of reference. (p. 7)

Problems encountered on patrol and discussion of goals are held during squad conferences which are used as an alternative to the traditional police roll call. Such procedures are an attempt to provide increasing feedback between supervisors and officers which will lead to an improved officer sense of participation and hopefully to greater productivity from the individual patrolman.

The San Diego project has major implications for our discussion of police and their relations with other helping agencies. The promise of this particular approach is that it encourages the patrol officer to become truly familiar with the environment and the individuals he comes into contact with every day. By the simple expedient of encouraging the officer to get out of his patrol car and talk to citizens, the officer should become more involved with the community. Through this involvement he should be better equipped to personally know helping agency personnel and to make more effective referrals regarding nonenforcement service requests.

Beyond this, the stated purpose of the San Diego project: "a humanistic orientation to a reasoned patrol practice based on beat accountability" (p. 17) speaks directly to the problems faced by the police forces of Newbarrow and Manford. Simply put, it is an effort to have the individual officer carry out his duties with an attitude of genuine concern for the human beings he encounters, rather than approaching his job in a purely mechanical manner, seeing the tasks he performs as just so many unconnected pieces of work.

Summary • The community conference model such as used in Newbarrow and Manford will not automatically translate expressions of goodwill into new policies and attitudes by either the police or their social agency counterparts. The San Diego Community Profile Project, however promising, still must stand the test of time and rigorous evaluation to determine its impact on police enforcement and nonenforcement service delivery.

However, the models of in-depth police-community contact here suggested hold more promise of bringing about genuine cooperation and providing full services for the ordinary citizen than countless sessions which deal in pieties and platitudes concerning "human relations."

❨ 4 ❩

Planning in
Police–Community
Relations

In Chapter 2 the implications of the full service model for policing were discussed. The present chapter will look at the ways in which the community perceives the police and their delivery of services to the community. Specifically, this chapter will deal with the citizens' attitudes toward the police of a medium-sized suburban city in the Northeast. Additionally, the issue of comprehensive planning for effective delivery of services will be further examined.

One might ask, "What do citizens' attitudes have to do with the ways in which the police function in the community?" The answer may seem simplistic on the surface, yet few departments are willing to concede that citizens' attitudes do have an impact. In part, the police are sworn to uphold the law. Theoretically, the community through its elected officials has established the rule of law in order to create harmony within the society. The police then, at least in theory, enforce the laws which are a reflection of the will of the community. This is immediately apparent in light of the 1972 Supreme Court decisions on pornography and community values. These decisions emphasized the importance of considering community feelings in determining whether a particular film, book, or play is pornographic. On a less abstract level, the police are employees of the community. They are paid to enforce the laws that the community has established. Therefore, it is appropriate, if not necessary, for the community to express their opinions on the behavior of the police within the community.

• THE VALUE OF
CONSUMER FEEDBACK

The idea of seeking consumer feedback might have a powerful impact on the way in which the police deliver their services. With respect to the full service model, members of the community should have the right to indicate what services are needed and desired. Allowing community members to participate with the police in deciding jointly what types of services are to be provided, as well as reviewing the current services offered, will create a sense of total community cooperation and responsibility for policing. And policing becomes easier with the support of the community. The following discussion examines a survey of citizens' attitudes toward the police, and considers the necessity for careful research in determining what services are afforded to the community.

Dudley D. Gourley (1974) here addresses himself to the use of the market analysis to determine what the public wants with respect to law enforcement. Gourley writes:

> The situation calls for shrewd market analysis from design *stem* [origin] to implementation in order to be successful in the tough and oftentimes hard-to-define areas of police service. As a result of the use of market analysis, new patterns of police/citizen cooperation will evolve, as well as new lines of communication with the public who will demand a share in the formulation of these innovative programs as part of its cooperation. (p. 16)

Gourley further comments:

> The public would have a part in what the police do for them, and why not? In that the public pays the taxes, it is similar to a group of shareholders making up a corporation. Like the shareholders who have a vote in the direction the corporation takes in the business world, so the public should have some control of the direction in which the police force goes. As a result, instead of fighting the police, the minorities and the average taxpayer will support the police because they will be getting the product they want, which is police service. (p. 16)

Fink and Sealy (1974), commenting on the need for more community participation in law enforcement, state:

> It is axiomatic among police that the less citizens have to do with the process of law enforcement, the better it is for the police—there is less interference as the police go about their work, less "second-guessing,"

less "control." The reverse is actually the case. The greater the citizen's involvement and participation in the criminal justice system, the easier it is for the police to request and receive compliance, support and comfort. Even tangential involvement is better than none. (p. 47)

Thus, consumer feedback, market analysis, and community participation in the criminal justice system are vitally important.

Impact of LEAA • With the creation of the Law Enforcement Assistance Administration in 1965, and the passage in 1968 of the Omnibus Crime Control and Safe Streets Act, millions of dollars in aid were made available to the police and other agencies in the criminal justice system. However, before such agencies could enjoy the benefits of the then newly passed legislation, planning and documentation were required by Federal authorities to show that a need existed within the local agency.

Today, planning and research within the agencies of the criminal justice system have become big business. Yet, planning for criminal justice has often taken place without adequately defining the problem within the particular setting. A good example may be found within the police-community relations milieu. It is a common experience for a police department to become committed to the "storefront" concept of PCR, only to be disillusioned when police are forced to close these operations as the novelty wears off and citizens fail to stop by and "rap" with officers on duty.

A more viable approach, it would seem, is to first identify and otherwise define the community's attitudes and opinions regarding police issues. Then, with the hard data in hand, the question of police-community relations, or other police problems, should be approached in a systematic manner. This type of consumer feedback can affect how the police approach and define problems within the community in order to plan programs necessary to solve the identified problems.

Thus, research and planning are necessary for effective police functioning within the community. Research and planning should occupy a high position in the list of priorities of the police. Sound planning includes the evaluation of existing programs as well as identification of problem areas not covered by existing programs.

• IDENTIFYING COMMUNITY NEEDS

Trojanowicz and Dixon (1974) suggest that comprehensive planning is necessary for:

1 · Establishing realistic goals

2 · Measuring accomplishments

3 · Meeting goals on schedule

4 · Justifying programs to the resource providers

5 · Matching goals and resources and applying acquired resources

6 · Defining and improving continued and subsequent programs

7 · Communicating to all concerned

8 · Motivating all concerned to the achievement of the stated goals. (p. 370)

The use of the community needs survey as a research and planning technique specifically points toward the establishment of realistic goals, and defining and improving subsequent programs.

Trojanowicz and Dixon further point out that in regard to police-community relations programs, research and planning are absolutely necessary. Police-community relations concepts, programs, and units are a relatively recent phenomenon in police organizations. Therefore, little research and evaluation has been undertaken about the necessity and/or effectiveness of PCR programs. Yet, without research and evaluation, successful approaches cannot be readily identified and dysfunctional programs eliminated.

Munro (1974) indicates that the classical model of planning includes four basic steps:

1 · Perception, identification and analysis of the problem

2 · Search for solutions

3 · Anticipation of the consequences of alternative solutions

4 · Selection of the solution, implementation, and feedback. (p. 164)

Thus, the police must:

1 · Perceive, identify, and analyze problems facing the establishment of a good relationship between the police and the community. Implied here is some form of data collection for the proper identification and analysis of the particular problem. What is the problem? Do we have the facts? What do they mean? All are questions that must be considered here;

2 · Search for and establish solutions based on the identified

problem. Solutions must be compatible with the data that has been collected and analyzed. How we can solve the problem is the consideration here;

3 · Anticipate the consequences or outcomes of the proposed solutions. What effects the solutions will have on both the police and the community, and which solution is best are the items of concern here;

4 · Implement the best solution and gather feedback (data) to see if the solution is working.

Planning is therefore necessary if the police organization is to change along with the community. By using the consumer feedback system, the police can plan to change and meet the subsequent needs within the community. Research and planning will aid the police in understanding the community and will supply the knowledge so necessary to provide good police service.

Grange (1974) comments:

Understanding and knowledge are the best tools for effective police work, especially when there is a question of better police-community relations. Violence gathers to itself only more violence; and if the police wish to be viewed as professionals, they must equip themselves with the best knowledge available. In that way, persuasion replaces force and professionalism along with public esteem increases. Law enforcement agencies are in a difficult position. They require society's cooperation, but at the present moment find themselves mistrusted and mistreated by the society they serve. The key to reversing this situation lies in the direction of more knowledge and a better grasp of the dynamics of conflict. (p. 36)

By utilizing a consumer feedback system and by careful research and planning, the police can gain such knowledge.

Further commenting on the planning process, Berkley (1975) states:

Successful planning requires information, a great deal of information. To begin with, the planners have to find out all they can about their own organization, its purposes and policies, its culture and characteristics, its strengths and weaknesses. Then they must find out what other organizations like their own are doing and what successes or setbacks these organizations are experiencing and why. At the same time they must also keep tabs on the doings and designs of organizations which are not like their own but which can affect their organization's activities in many ways. And finally, planners have to know the total environment in which their organization functions. They must acquire an awareness of what is going on in society and an appreciation of how the changes that are occurring in society may influence their organization's future. Thus, before anything else, planning is an information-gathering function. (p. 335)

A well designed community needs survey is one means of gathering consumer feedback. Such feedback can achieve the following objectives for the police:

1 · It can be an invaluable tool for police planning, not only in police-community relations, but in other areas as well.

2 · It can serve as an opportunity for ventilation of public feelings and attitudes toward the police.

3 · It can facilitate genuine communication between the police and the community, thus performing a valuable police-community relations function.

A number of studies to identify and otherwise define problems within the community have been conducted in the last several years. Consumer surveys designed to reveal variations within a community and to enable the police to concentrate their efforts on areas of low satisfaction have been reported by Furstenberg and Wellford (1973), Finckenhauer (1970), and Reiss (1971).

• THE COMMUNITY NEEDS SURVEY: A MODEL

The data gathered in the model Community Needs Survey were collected by means of an interview technique with the residents of a medium-sized, suburban city in the Northeast. The questionnaire employed in this study was designed to elicit several types of information. First, information regarding the demographic background of the participants was obtained; this consisted of questions about race, sex, income, occupational status, and dwelling space. Second, information concerning beliefs about general police functioning was sought. This included attitudes toward police service, crime problems, and suggestions for change.

If the results of this survey were to be meaningful for future police planning, then randomness of the sample was essential. Thus, a rather complex formula was designed to enable the researchers to choose the participants from the police sector divisions of the city.

Objectives of the Community Needs Survey • This survey was designed specifically to achieve the following objectives:

1 · To determine the needs, wants, desires, and expectations of the community with regard to police service
2 · To identify the types of crimes of most concern to the community and focus general patterns of such crimes in the community
3 · To evaluate in general the services of the local police department as observed by the community.

In addition, some secondary purposes were incorporated into the survey:

1 · To obtain demographic data for future police planning
2 · To facilitate police-community contact
3 · To involve the community directly in police matters.

In general, there were two separate but related goals for this survey: first, to assess the value of such a survey as a tool for police departments in dealing with police-community relations problems; and second, to assess the public attitudes toward police behavior in the community. If the information gathered was meaningful and useful, and if the citizens were willing and able to provide the requested information, then this technique would prove a valuable part of a police planning program.

The data presented in Tables 4.1, 4.2, 4.3, and 4.4 represent the distribution of age, sex, race, and income for the total sample. There were approximately 15 respondents for each of the 10 sectors of the city.

Table 4.1   Age Distribution

Years	N	%
15-24	14	9
25-34	32	22
35-44	28	19
45-54	36	24
55-64	26	17
65-	13	9
Total	149	100

Table 4.2   Sex Distribution

Sex	N	%
Male	73	49
Female	76	51
Total	149	100

Table 4.3   Race Distribution

Race	N	%
Black	27	18
White	122	82
Total	149	100

Table 4.4   Income Distribution

Income	N	%
Under 10K	38	26
10-14K	42	28
15-19K	12	8
20K-	3	2
No Data	54	36
Total	149	100

It can be seen by the data in the tables that the sample was probably not unlike many other communities located in proximity to a larger urban area. These figures reflect quite accurately the various proportions of the known variables within the community. The one exception is the racial breakdown. The 18 percent figure for the minority respondents is approximately double the actual proportion. The discrepancy is probably based on the make-up of the patrol sectors from which the sample was randomly selected.

Several questions were concerned with the overall functioning of the police in the community. To the question, "Have you called the police department in the last year?", 48% or 73 of those interviewed had called the police department for one reason or another. Out of the 48% who had called the police, 50% called fewer than four times, with the remaining 49% making more than four calls per year. Inquiries about the reason for the calls found that 25% of those calls were related to crimes or accidents. It is significant that 75% of the calls were other than law enforcement related.

These results suggest that the use of a community needs survey will help the police department in the planning of its services to the community. The knowledge that 75% of the calls to this department deal with other than law enforcement activities suggest the need for alternative methods of defining the police function within the community.

A Measure of Police Responsiveness • An important aspect of police-community relations is the way in which police respond to citizens. Those who had called the police were asked, "When you called the police department, how did the officer answer your call?" Of citizens with such contact, 50% reported that the officer was very concerned to polite; 18% reported average responses; and 9% reported brisk or unconcerned contacts. Twenty-three respondents answered that the contacts were other than the categories listed or gave no response. This data may be interpreted by stating that there were 68% positive or average responses, and 9% negative responses, with 23 of the responses unable to be categorized.

In order to evaluate the general perception of the public toward police services, the following question was asked: "In your opinion, the Metropolitan Police Department in offering its services is _____."

Table 4.5   Rating of Police Services

	(N)	(%)
Excellent	45	30
Good	46	31
Average	23	15
Fair	7	5
Poor	8	6
No Response	20	13
Totals	149	100

All respondents were asked to answer this and the following three questions regardless of whether or not they had called the police in the last year. As can be seen in Table 4.5, an overwhelming majority (76%) of those interviewed felt that the Metropolitan Police Department in offering its services was excellent to average, while only 11% felt that it was fair to poor.

With regard to police conduct, participants were asked, "Is the Metropolitan Police Department fair, honest, average, dishonest, or brutal?"

Table 4.6   Police Conduct

	(N)	(%)
Fair	53	37
Honest	47	32
Average	13	8
Dishonest	14	9
Brutal	1	1
No Response	8	5
Other	13	8
Totals	149	100

Again, the data shows a definitely positive perception of the police.

To determine where citizens' fear and concerns are focused, respondents were asked to answer the open-ended question: "What do you believe is the most probable crime or police related problem that could happen to you in your neighborhood?" Results indicate that robbery with 13%, juvenile-related with 13%, breaking and entering with 12%, and vandalism with 10% are the types of crimes that the respondents feel could happen to them in their neighborhoods. Further responses range from concern over homicide to runaways. Out of this data, it is interesting to note that 23% of the respondents were concerned with vandalism and juvenile-related problems. For a community which is planning to undertake a police-community relations program, these facts indicate a need to direct a considerable portion of that effort toward youth.

Public views of the direction in which the police department should move were sampled with the following question: "What changes, if any, would you suggest for the Metropolitan Police Department?" Results showed that more patrol with 19% of the responses, no changes with 9%, and more policemen with 3% were the significant responses. Marginal responses ranged from less political control to emphasis on the juvenile delinquent. Perhaps the most interesting note is that many of the respondents wanted more patrol activities on the part of the police. Indications are that 19 percent of the sampled population thought the police department should increase its activities in this area.

The Survey in Detail: A Breakdown by Sector • The survey data lends itself effectively to a more detailed analysis. The following tables represent the sector division of the community matched with the attitude variables. The sector division follows the police breakdown of beats for the community. It should be noted that Sector 27, although not a true sector, represents a special sample of the population. This sample was drawn from the official Case Incident Reports of the police, with the desire of surveying individuals who were known to have had official contact with the police in the last year for one reason or another. The purpose was to select a special sample to see how their responses would match with others in the survey.

Table 4.7 indicates the reason for calling the police by sector. Our data indicates that out of the total calls throughout each sector, 10% deal directly with crime problems, and 7% fall within the "Combination" category with a crime response. However, 24% of the other single category calls and 4% of the calls within the "Combination" category without a crime response deal with nonenforcement service duties. Basing our conclusion on 100%, and dropping the "No Response" category, the law enforcement calls would comprise 36% of the total, with the remaining 64% being general service-oriented duties. This reinforces our suggestion stated in Chapter 2 that the police role should be viewed in a total service concept rather than enforcement dominated because police spend relatively little time on purely law enforcement tasks.

Table 4.8 reports how the responding police officer acted as perceived by the individual who had called the police. A "Combination" category exists with positive and negative responses. Analysis shows that 68% indicated a positive response from "Very Concerned" to "Average" and 9% indicated a negative response.

Table 4.9 summarizes the responses by sector to the question, "In your opinion, the Metropolitan Police Department in offering its services is _____?" Responses show that 94 or 76% of the participants indicated a positive response (Excellent to Average) and 15 or 10% replied negatively.

Table 4.10 reports the data for the opinion question, "Is the Metropolitan Police Department fair, honest, average, dishonest, or brutal?" by sector breakdown. Again there is a "Combination" category with both positive and negative responses. Analysis shows that 76% rate the police

Table 4.7 Frequency and Percent of the Responses to the Question: "What was the Reason for your Call?" by Sector

Sector	Crime	Accident	Sickness	Other	Combination*	No Response
1	1 (8%)			4 (33%)	1 (8%)	6 (50%)
2	1 (8%)	1 (8%)		3 (23%)		8 (62%)
3	2 (14%)		1 (7%)	1 (7%)		10 (67%)
4	1 (6%)			3 (18%)	4 (24%)	9 (53%)
5				2 (13%)	1 (6%)	13 (81%)
6	3 (15%)			5 (25%)	3 (15%)	9 (45%)
7			1 (7%)		1 (7%)	12 (86%)
8	3 (20%)		1 (7%)	3 (20%)		8 (53%)
9	1 (7%)		1 (7%)	4 (27%)	2 (14%)	7 (47%)
27 (Special)	3 (25%)		2 (17%)	3 (25%)	2 (17%)	2 (17%)

N = 149

* The "Combination" category represents a grouping of the separate categories of crime, accident, sickness, and other. It is possible for an individual to have called the police department four times in the past year for different reasons represented by the four categories. These categories are mutually exclusive; the "Other" category represents responses ranging from questions about parking violations to questions about directions for street locations.

Table 4.8 Frequency and Percent of Response to the Question: "How did the Officer Respond to you?" by Sector

Sector	Very Concerned 1	Polite 2	Average 3	Brisk 4	Totally Unconcerned 5	No Response 0	Other* +	Other* −
1	1 (8%)	2 (17%)	3 (25%)			4 (33%)	2 (17%)	
2						9 (69%)	4 (31%)	
3	3 (20%)		2 (13%)			10 (67%)		
4	1 (6%)	4 (24%)	2 (12%)	1 (6%)		9 (53%)		
5	1 (6%)					14 (88%)	1 (6%)	
6		5 (25%)	2 (10%)	3 (15%)	1 (5%)	9 (45%)		
7	1 (7%)	2 (14%)	2 (14%)			8 (57%)	1 (7%)	
8	5 (33%)	1 (7%)				9 (60%)		
9	1 (7%)	3 (20%)	1 (7%)			9 (60%)	1 (7%)	
27 (Special)	1 (8%)	2 (17%)	1 (8%)			2 (17%)	4 (33%)	2 (17%)

N = 149

* Other–these responses did not fall into the major categories but could be classified as essentially positive or negative.

Table 4.9 Frequency and Percent of Response to the Question: "In your opinion, the Metropolitan Police Department in offering its services is _____." by Sector

Sector	Excellent 1	Good 2	Average 3	Fair 4	Poor 5	No Response 0
1	4 (33%)	7 (58%)	1 (8%)			
2	8 (62%)	3 (23%)		1 (8%)		1 (8%)
3	3 (20%)	1 (7%)		1 (7%)		10 (72%)
4	1 (6%)	5 (29%)	8 (47%)		3 (18%)	
5	4 (25%)	6 (38%)	5 (31%)	1 (6%)		
6	1 (5%)	5 (25%)	6 (30%)	3 (15%)	5 (25%)	
7	4 (29%)	8 (57%)		1 (7%)		1 (7%)
8	5 (33%)	1 (7%)	1 (7%)			8 (53%)
9	7 (47%)	7 (47%)	1 (7%)			
27 (Special)	8 (67%)	3 (25%)	1 (8%)			

N = 149

Table 4.10   Frequency and Percent of Responses to the Question:
"Is the Metropolitan Police Department _____?" by Sector

Sector	Fair 1	Honest 2	Average 3	Dishonest 4	Brutal 5	No Response 0	Other +	Other −
1	4 (33%)	3 (25%)		4 (33%)		1 (8%)		
2	5 (38%)	1 (8%)	2 (15%)			1 (8%)	4 (31%)	
3	9 (60%)	3 (20%)	1 (7%)			1 (7%)	1 (7%)	
4	2 (12%)	9 (53%)	2 (12%)	4 (24%)				
5	7 (44%)	6 (38%)				2 (13%)	1 (6%)	
6	3 (15%)	9 (45%)	3 (15%)	3 (15%)	1 (5%)			1 (5%)
7	6 (43%)	4 (29%)		4 (29%)				
8	8 (53%)	5 (33%)	1 (7%)			1 (7%)		
9	5 (33%)	5 (33%)	2 (13%)			1 (7%)	2 (13%)	
27 (Special)	5 (42%)	2 (17%)	2 (17%)			1 (8%)	2 (17%)	

N = 149

from Fair to Average, and 10% indicate a negative response (Dishonest to Brutal).

Sector 6: What a More Detailed Analysis Suggests • Negative responses are something more than simple unfavorable feedback. They are, if accepted and understood, a source of vital information for the perceptive police planner, administrator, or line officer. A summary of the negative responses for Sector #6 may be found in Table 4.11.

Table 4.11   A Summary of Negative Responses from Sector #6

A. Frequency and Percentage of Responses to the Question:
"How did the officer respond to you?"

	1 Very Concerned	2 Polite	3 Average	4 Brisk	5 Total Unconcern	0 No Response	Other + −
Sector #6	5 (25%)	2 (10%)	3 (15%)	1 (5%)	9 (45%)		

B. Frequency and Percentage of Responses to the Question:
"In your opinion the Metropolitan Police Department in offering its services is _____."

	1 Excellent	2 Good	3 Average	4 Fair	5 Poor	0 No Response
Sector #6	1 (5%)	5 (25%)	6 (30%)	3 (15%)	5 (25%)	

C. Frequency and Percentage of Responses to the Question:
"Is the Metropolitan Police Department _____?"

	1 Fair	2 Honest	3 Average	4 Dishonest	5 Brutal	0 No Response
Sector #6	3 (15%)	9 (45%)	3 (15%)	3 (15%)	1 (5%)	1 (5%)

In considering the question, 'How did the officer respond to you?", the value of 4 means "Brisk" and the value of 5 means "Totally Unconcerned." Table 4.12 reports the demographic variables associated with each response.

Table 4.12   Demographic Characteristics of Individuals from Sector #6 Responding Negatively to the Question: "How Did the Officer Respond to You?"

Re-sponse	Age	Sex	Race	Income	Occup.	Dwelling Space
4	45-54	F	B	Under $10K	Unempl.	Rent–Apt.
4	25-34	M	B	No resp.	No resp.	Own–Home
4	15-24	M	B	Under $10K	Semi-skl.	Rent–Apt.
5	45-54	M	B	Under $10K	No resp.	Rent–Apt.

Table 4.13 reports the demographic breakdown of responses to the question, "In your opinion, the Metropolitan Police Department in offering its service is _____?" A response of 4 means "Fair" and a response of 5 means "Poor."

Table 4.13   Demographic Characteristics of Individuals from Sector #6 Responding Negatively to the Question: In Your Opinion, the Metropolitan Police Department in Offering Its Services is _____?"

Re-sponse	Age	Sex	Race	Income	Occup.	Dwelling Space
4	35-44	F	B	No resp.	No resp.	Rent–Apt.
4	35-44	F	W	$10-15K	Manager	Own–Home
5	45-54	F	B	Under $10K	Unempl.	Rent–Apt.
5	45-54	F	B	Under $10K	No resp.	Rent–Apt.
5	25-34	M	B	No resp.	No resp.	Own–Home
5	35-44	M	B	No resp.	Unskilled	Rent–Apt.
5	15-24	F	B	Under $10K	Semi-skl.	Rent–Apt.

The negative responses for the question, "Is the Metropolitan Police Department _____:" are found in Table 4.14, with a response of 4 meaning "Dishonest" and 5 meaning "Brutal."

Table 4.14   Demographic Characteristics of Individuals from Sector #6 Responding Negatively to the Question: "Is the Metropolitan Police Department _____?"

Re-sponse	Age	Sex	Race	Income	Occup.	Dwelling Space
4	45-54	M	B	$10-15K	Manager	Own—Home
4	25-34	F	W	No resp.	Manager	Rent—Apt.
4	45-54	F	W	Under $10K	Retired	Rent—Apt.
5	45-54	F	B	Under $10K	Unempl.	Rent—Apt.
Comb. 3/5	15-24	F	B	Under $10K	Semi-skl.	Rent—Apt.

Although the responses found in Tables 4.12, 4.13, and 4.14 do not represent any statistical significance in terms of the total response for each question, they do have a bearing on the scope of the survey and should be considered when planning for police service for Sector #6. It is clear from the tabular data that the majority of the respondents were black, living in rented apartments, with incomes of less than or equal to $10,000 per year. Perhaps since 81% of the respondents with negative replies were black, a different approach may need to be taken with the black citizens of Sector #6.

Other studies have shown a difference in the intensity of encounters with police between black and white communities. Jacob (1971) examined perceptions of injustice and reports that the way people view the police differs within two particular communities. Campbell and Schuman (1970), in a study of attitudes toward the police, find that blacks are far more likely than whites to have had unfavorable experiences with the police. Thus, it seems vital that the police identify feelings and problems of certain groups in order to plan police service effectively.

•   SOME CONCLUSIONS

Generally, the data indicates that the community studied has a strong amount of support and respect for police functioning, a factor we suggest is not uncommon for most similar police departments. And perhaps this indicates that the police should begin to reevaluate their own perceptions of community attitudes. While there are negative attitudes present, they tend to be expressed by a small percentage of the community with certain identifiable characteristics. Even though there are only a small number of negative responses, one should not discount their validity. On the contrary, one needs to know demographically who and where these responses are coming from in order to plan activities necessary to overcome the apparent problems.

By using a survey of this nature, police planning units are able to clearly define general problem areas within the community, as well as zero in on certain segments within the population. This capability is particularly important for urban and suburban police departments where great diversity exists among the population. By clearly defining problem areas and target populations, the police will find themselves in the position of being able to offer services which are specifically tailored to meet the defined wants and needs of the community.

The use of the community needs survey thus fulfills two main objectives: it allows for consumer feedback on police functioning within the community, and it allows the police to clearly identify areas of citizens' concerns and to plan the necessary action. The community survey is a viable and legitimate tool for police use, particularly in the area of police-community relations.

• THE NEED FOR POLICE PLANNING

Wilson (1952) discusses some further considerations of the planning process and the police organization. He defines planning as the process of developing a method or procedure or an arrangement of parts to facilitate the achievement of a defined objective. He further indicates there are several considerations in a plan that are of great value to the planners.

1 · A plan implements policy and clarifies it by precisely defining an immediate objective or purpose. Plans in police-community relations serve to clearly define for the police, and for the community, the particular policies the police have as an organization with respect to certain problems.

2 · A plan serves as a guide or reference in both training and performance. Since the plan clearly shows what the police policy is in respect to certain problems, the training of police officers

in the area of police-community relations will be guided by the policies of the organization. Plans also aid the department in evaluation of men in the field; evaluation of line performance of the plan is an important element in its successful implementation. Plans largely shape the way in which police respond to the problem area, and ultimately this performance may be evaluated in order to guarantee the success of the plan.

3 · The planning process gives continued attention to the improvement of practices and procedures. Planning and the implementation of plans will show where further work or emphasis needs to be placed. Thus, plans may serve to keep the police aware of the need for constant improvement and change.

4 · A plan enables a check on accomplishments in order to evaluate the success of meeting goals set by the plan.

5 · Wise planning assures the most effective and economical use of resources. Because of the extreme costs for both men and equipment, it is imperative that the police utilize their resources in a planned fashion.

There are still other considerations in regard to police planning and police-community relations. Johnson (1975) contends that police-community relations efforts have been largely ineffectual because of a lack of structural changes within the organization. These changes are necessary to facilitate the functioning of good police-community relations efforts.

The police and others have been very astute in planning strategies, techniques, and programs to improve and foster good police-community relations. Yet, planning efforts directed at the internal organizational functioning of a department have long been ignored. Police have generally resisted, according to the Johnson viewpoint, police-community relations efforts, because of a lack of organizational—structural changes to support and facilitate these programs. It is impossible to change police practices without structure change. Doig (1968) comments:

. . . the problem of changing police practices is not only a matter of identifying proposals which appear reasonably helpful in meeting current nationwide issues. In addition, someone—and ultimately the elected officials and police commissioners of individual cities—must cope with two additional, interrelated questions: How can such proposals be carefully evaluated in terms of their impact on the city and the police department —so that those that will yield significant net benefits can be separated from those which will generate more problems than benefits? And, how can the stronger proposals be implemented? (p. 396)

What is necessary is not only problem or proposal identification, but also some genuine planning for change in order to gain the "significant net benefit." Not only is it necessary to plan new strategies and programs, but it is also necessary to devise plans to accomodate these "changes" within the structure of the department. Thus Berkley (1975) writes:

Planning also has much to offer public administrators. Here, as elsewhere, planning permits the organization not only to anticipate and prepare for changes but also, at least to some extent, to select and shape such changes as will come. Planning offers a way of institutionalizing vision and stabilizing innovation. It permits the future to shape the past, rather than the opposite. An organization that plans is an organization that, at least theoretically, has accepted the value and necessity of change. (p. 332)

In summary then, research and planning are vital necessities for the police, particularly in the area of police-community relations. Only by knowing what is needed within the community will the police be able to deal effectively with and offer the proper services to the community. Echoing this same theme, Germann (1968) comments:

Police planning and research has a genuine and proper role in police-community relations. It accomplishes much now by promoting efficiency in general police administration, supervision, and operations. It can accomplish a great deal more in the future by interesting itself in promoting morality and legality, and by assisting in the elimination of any harmful attitudes and practices of the public which contribute to the maintenance of the gap between the public and the police.

In that fashion, the police planning and research unit will contribute to the achievement of ordered liberty in a democratic society, to responsible and responsive policing, and to community acceptance of the fact that the police are the public, and the public are the police—a unity dedicated to the Common Good. (p. 397)

〔 5 〕

The PCR Role

Earlier in the book the specific tasks of PCR units and individual PCR officers were briefly examined. Any discussion of the role of police-community relations should begin with a simple question: Is it necessary or desirable to establish such a unit or to detach an officer to perform police-community relations tasks?

We have already suggested that a genuine police-community relations effort involves significantly more than "doing something," such as automatically creating a special unit to process or deal directly with a wide range of nonenforcement service concerns. By using a form of community needs survey or other such vehicle, a police administrator should determine the specific relationship existing between the public and the police before developing a special PCR unit.

There are a variety of ways of determining how people really feel about police services. A Community Needs Survey and the community conference are two such vehicles for obtaining community feedback. Other possibilities are numerous. The police, through a series of meetings with appropriate civic and social groups, can learn much about community reactions to their services. This type of sampling process should also include individual community leaders, not necessarily those immediately perceived as being the "big people" in the community, but rather those who influence, often in a quiet, unstructured way, important segments of community opinion. Simply put, the corner grocer may have a much more sensitive appraisal of community or neighborhood feelings about police services than the local clergyman, whose activities and reach may not extend to as broad a segment of the community.

There is no set format to gather this type of information. Various settings may be employed. Formal, publicly announced meetings could be called for the express purpose of gathering public reaction, or the process might consist of informal, somewhat unstructured, yet systematic interviews with both groups and individuals. The business of evaluation, whether performed in house or through the use of an outside consultant, usually stirs uneasiness in any group of individuals, be they police, educators, or businessmen. In the final analysis, it seems that very few people like to go through this process, for there is always a strong possibility that the feedback that we desire to receive will not be given.

• THE POLICE ADMINISTRATOR'S TASK

Therefore, the first step in a genuine appraisal of police-community relations is often the most difficult one for the administrator to take—namely exposing himself and his department to public criticism and comment. Yet, if an honest evaluation of police-public interaction is to be made, this step must be taken freely and in good faith. It is equally important that the opinions, feelings, and reactions of line officers and middle management police personnel be sought in an open fashion. How do these men really see their jobs? What types of satisfactions and dissatisfactions exist? How may we develop a more positive job outlook for the rank and file officer?

Again, it is important that a diversity of views be sought during these in-house discussions. Not only should there be a good cross section of all ranks represented, but also it is important for the administrator to incorporate in the discussion process those line and middle management individuals who mold department opinion. As with the civilian population, the most obvious individuals are not necessarily the most appropriate persons from whom to seek opinions. For instance, the president of the local police union may well indeed reflect the views of most rank and file officers. However, the perceptive administrator will also attempt to identify other members of his department who informally mold departmental reactions to official policies and reflect rank and file views.

At some point it may be highly desirable to bring representatives of both groups together for a series of meetings that will fully probe any issues that have arisen and provide the administrator with an overview of both reactions and interaction. As suggested earlier in our discussion of several social service conference meetings, the best way to bring about a real exchange is to avoid a one-shot session and instead develop a series of meetings, preferably guided by a skilled moderator. It is important, in this information gathering process to avoid holding meetings just for the sake of meetings. Some clearly defined objectives, issues, or articulated concerns should serve as a focal point for discussion.

It is only through a systematic process of information seeking that a rational decision can be made about the establishment of a PCR unit and its possible goals. We would strongly suggest that if gaps are found in the everyday interaction between citizens and police, all other alternatives should be explored before a separate unit is established. The reasons are fairly straightforward. A solution to the lack of positive interaction may simply be a continuation of the earlier discussions between citizens and police, using a rotating group of officers and citizens so that a cross section of total community opinion and reactions may be obtained. The administrator may elect to institute a revised training program for both veteran and new personnel that would deal with some of the issues raised by both officers and citizens. A third alternative might involve more frequent communication between the chief as overall administrator and various community leaders identified during the information gathering process. This might include directors of various service agencies as well as nonprofessional citizen representatives. The total amount of time devoted to these discussions need not be extensive, but in order to assess the most appropriate ways of developing closer police-civilian ties all these steps should be considered.

Assuming that the administrator has weighed all these possibilities, he may well decide that a specialized unit which would perform all these tasks both in house and in relation to the total community would be most appropriate. Three basic considerations are involved: setting specific, achievable goals; defining the type of personnel needed to carry out these goals; and establishing a set of evaluation tools to measure unit progress.

• PCR UNIT FUNCTIONS

The PCR unit should be envisioned as performing both line and staff functions in its initial phase of operation. These operations will, of course, vary with the size of the community involved. We would strongly suggest, however, that over the long term, the PCR unit should be seen as performing staff rather than line or service delivery functions.

Klyman (1974) in a survey of 67 PCR units, reported that units included in his study spent the following proportions of their time providing a variety of services.

**Table 5.1   The Mean Percentages of Time Spent by
Police-Community Relations Units On the
Various Kinds of Services**

Services	Of Total Police Community Relations Unit Manpower Resources, % Manhours Currently Expended	Projection of % of Manhours that Will Be Expended Next Year
Office management of police-community relations unit office	11.96	11.39
Public information and press relations	8.77	9.17
Police-school liaison and/or teaching	18.47	19.88
Participation in departmental training programs	5.05	6.59
Handling citizen complaints against police officers	1.72	1.53
Recruiting	4.08	4.19
Coordinating social services with community service agencies	11.16	11.98
Research in police-community relations programming	5.27	5.80
Delivery services through store-front center(s)	5.18	5.58
Delivery of youth services	10.88	8.88
Delivery of counseling services to citizens	9.38	9.52
Other	8.08	5.49

Reprinted from: Fred I. Klyman, The Police-Community Relations Survey: a
quantitative inventory of services and work units, *Journal of Police Science
and Administration*, 1974, 2, p. 79.

Although Klyman's study involved PCR units in larger communities
(only eight of the sample cities were under 100,000 population), his
study provides some indication of the types of duties currently being
carried out by a fairly broad spectrum of units.

Considering our previous comment concerning appropriate PCR activities, a disproportionate amount of unit time appears to have been spent on such activities as police-school liaison and delivery of youth services. Unit time seems to be underutilized in the development of in-depth community dialog at all levels. Certainly this is the major thrust of the PCR unit—to provide both command and line officers with a true understanding of citizen expectations. The units surveyed also appear to have spent inadequate time in the areas of recruitment and training of new officers. The PCR unit, with its close ties to the community, should play a vital role in the identification and development of those candidates likely to be interested in policing as a career, who have a commitment to the concept of the total service function.

In general, surveyed PCR programs seem to be overemphasizing services to youth, which accounted for 29.4% of survey group man-hours expended. Delivery of services need not be handled by a PCR unit, particularly efforts aimed at a limited segment of the community. Indeed, these services could and should be handled by properly trained line personnel who are sensitive to the needs of the total community.

• GOALS FOR A TOTAL COMMUNITY EFFORT

Recommended goals for a PCR unit include a substantial involvement in the following areas: establishing continuing contact with citizen groups; initial provision of highly specialized direct services such as crisis intervention; participation in training and recruiting; and carrying out a continuing program of public information using the full range of available media.

The basic priority for a PCR unit should be the establishment of a continuing flow of comment, reactions, and information between the PCR unit and appropriate citizen groups. Klyman's (1974) study reveals that only 25% of those departments participating in the study had established a community relations, citizens advisory committee composed of ordinary citizens. The Task Force on Police of the National Advisory Commission on Criminal Justice Standards and Goals (1973) has noted:

Such councils, if truly representative, can serve both as an effective means of determining the community's needs and expectations and as a forum for explaining and encouraging acceptance of policies developed in response to those needs. (p. 30)

The Task Force further noted:

> The success of community advisory councils, both formal and informal, depends largely upon how well the members represent the community, and upon the willingness of police agencies to consider and act on their recommendations. Police agencies should attempt to insure the independence of the council and be receptive to its recommendations. (p. 30)

It would seem mandatory that this type of continuing relationship be undertaken if the PCR unit is to be really involved in the business of establishing dialogue and mutual cooperation between citizens and the police. Without such a contact, the PCR concept is built on sand.

The provision of specific, clearly defined information to the public concerning police programs and policies is an important potential task for newly organized PCR units. It should be noted that this type of duty differs sharply from the conventional public relations approach of continuous, superficial participation in various civic events.

• TRAINING:
A SPECIAL CONCERN

One of the most appropriate concerns for a meaningful PCR effort should be that unit staff is significantly involved in the training and development of personnel. If not doing the actual training, staff should be in close communication with the department training officers to develop innovative techniques that support the growth of the community service concept both in terms of recruits and veteran personnel. To date only a fraction of time of most police academy and in-service training programs has been devoted to that area broadly defined as human relations or interpersonal relations training.

As Reese (1973) has noted:

> The total recruit training format for large cities remains characterized by allocating the preponderance of training time to imparting skills in those tasks which are necessary to crime suppression and investigation. This favors the martial arts as they pertain to the war on crime. (p. 264)

Perhaps the most pressing issue for the PCR team regarding training is whether a little bit of human relations training or police community relations instruction is more dangerous than no training at all. Certainly the traditional stand-up lecture format offered as just another routine part of the overall training program at an in-service institute or training academy is highly unlikely to begin the process of changing attitudes of officers.

What is needed is a breakaway from the traditional format to a more individualized small group discussion experience, heavily interlaced with audio-visual material that clearly and specifically illustrates some of the human behavior problems that an officer is likely to face in his role of both enforcer and peacekeeper. Role playing of certain crisis situations can also be an informative experience for the officer, provided the sessions are led by an individual who has sound credentials in the area of human behavior. The PCR unit should seek to ensure that what is presented is something more than just a token gesture to placate those who feel that the police officer must be exposed to human relations training. There is much more value in systematic, continuing, in-service training which underscores and draws on the line officer's experience.

Here the small group session as described by Toch, Grant and Galvin (1975) while working with the Oakland, California Police Department, would seem to have major implications for other departments, even those of small to medium size. The basis of the Oakland project involved a lengthy series of working meetings with small groups of line officers who had experienced violent situations in their everyday tasks and had found difficulty in dealing effectively with such encounters. Toch *et al.* suggest that "participation models" produce change more completely and permanently than other styles of training.

Again, the success of any such ongoing program of staff development rests with the chief executive officer of the department. Something beyond tokenism is required. It should be made clear to all personnel that a high priority is placed on such in-service training and that built in evaluation yardsticks will be used to measure long term training impact.

Obviously the recruitment of individuals who are interested in carrying out police duties with a community-centered concern is of prime importance to the unit if its overall mission is to be accomplished. Therefore it would seem logical that the unit director or designated member should have some direct participation in the screening and selection of new recruits.

Every new officer who is unable to carry out his duties in a highly skilled fashion or is unable to handle the responsibilities or accept the gaff of police work presents a potential police-community relations problem. A vigorous selection process followed by an innovative, imaginative training program should be a key part of the police-community relations program.

Summary • In sum, the tasks of a PCR unit should not center on service delivery (except in the sole instance of crisis intervention work) but rather should provide both command and line personnel with a continuing flow of feedback and comment from citizens that will lead to the strengthening and enhancement of existing department policies. The second major task for PCR is to help both citizens and police administrators to define the pressing enforcement—service oriented needs of the community; needs to which the department will be expected to respond.

• SOME
PITFALLS

There are certain tasks that are not appropriate for a PCR unit. Establishing communications links with the community does not mean that the PCR unit or officer is to serve as an undercover agent or intelligence officer. While common sense would dictate that the PCR officer will not sit idly by if he receives information regarding the possible commission of an illegal act, or details which would result in the halting of criminal activity, he should not deliberately snoop for such information.

The key to the effectiveness of a PCR officer is the individual's ability to develop credibility in the community. This means that such an individual has to possess or develop a high sensitivity to the feelings of community residents. Brown (1970) relates how one officer handled a sensitive situation:

> I developed a good understanding with all organizations in the city, especially the militant groups. I am invited to all of their meetings. It is understood that I am a policeman, representing the police department. It is also understood that if they have something to discuss which they don't want the police to know about, they can just ask me to leave. This had occurred several times. It solves my problem since if what they discussed gets out, they can't blame me. It takes me off the spot and also takes them off the spot. (p. 183)

There is another aspect of credibility—namely that the ordinary citizen must have reasonable confidence that the PCR officer's position is one with some real clout within the particular police organization. Therefore it is vital that the police administrator stress to the public and all officers that the director of the PCR unit will have the freedom to make full and frank recommendations which will be examined and discussed in detail on all occasions. The Task Force on Police (1973) has recommended that "the unit should be no more than one step removed from the chief executive in the chain of command" (p. 29).

Clearly a PCR unit faces major problems within department ranks. From the line officer's point of view it is vital that the unit be seen as having direct practical value to his everyday tasks. It would be very easy to misinterpret the activities of the unit as being either to seek complaints from citizens concerning fellow officers, or, at the opposite extreme, to provide officers with the opportunity to divert difficult or unpopular tasks into the hands of unit members.

• CASE STUDIES

Just what are legitimate service activities for a PCR unit—particularly in providing direct services to clients? The following cases present actual situations as handled and recorded (verbatim) by PCR officers in a medium-sized city. The names of the actual participants have been changed.

Case One: Unwanted Elderly Tenant

Report of Investigation • The complainant came to the Community Relations Office with Mrs. Helpish, Social Worker from the Family Service Agency, who referred Mr. Sarrick for assistance by the Police Department. The problem centered around Mr. Sarrick feeling sorry for Mrs. Blist and moving her into his home because he assumed that she was a mistreated elderly person some 3 months ago. Since moving into the home, Mrs. Blist who is legally blind in one eye, has become a nuisance and very nerve shattering to be involved with. Mr. Sarrick is at the point of leaving his own home unless Mrs. Blist is removed. He admitted that he moved the woman into the home without the approval of his wife. Mrs. Blist has a sister, Mrs. Dew, who refuses to become involved. A daughter, Mrs. Darst of New Sedgewick, whom I could not reach. She also has a nephew, Alfred Eller, West Ivoryville, who agreed to make the necessary arrangements to get Mrs. Blist out of the home on Saturday, December 30, at 9:00 A.M. A Mr. Moller who operated a boarding house for elderly people at 130 Middle St., Middleville, will come down to Isselburg to pick up the woman.

It has been requested by Mrs. Helpish and Mrs. Blist that Police Officers be at the Sarrick home, 2nd floor, on Saturday, 9:00 A.M. to make it possible for Mrs. Blist to feel secure as she leaves the home.

Mrs. Helpish was assured that an officer would be at the Sarrick address at 9:00 A.M. on Saturday, December 30.

Discussion • Could this matter have been handled in a more efficient manner by the PCR unit? For instance, was it really necessary for the unit, in effect, to perform the duties of the private agency social worker? Perhaps the best method of handling this incident would have been for the unit commander to have indicated that a policeman would be provided at the time of the elderly tenant's departure. At the same time the social worker might have been taken aside and counseled about the specific goals of the PCR unit and how the unit might be of appropriate help to the agency in the future.

Case Two: Rent Dispute

Report of Investigation • The complainant stated that in the process of apartment hunting she had given deposits to (1) Mrs. Mease, Town St. $10.00—and to (2) Mr. Dills, Court St. $20.00. She further stated she found a third rent which was the best choice of the three. Returning to #1 she asked for a return of her deposit. #1 stated she would return the deposit on Saturday 5-18-68. #2 told the complainant that he could only return $10.00 of her deposit as the other ten was used in repairs. I explained to Mrs. Rentall that the Police Department did not usually get involved in Civil matters and this to the best of my knowledge was by no means a Police matter. I did speak to Mr. Dills and explained that in no way was the call official but I would like to hear his story. He stated that he would return the ten, rather than cause anyone any trouble. Complainant satisfied—case closed.

Discussion • In this particular instance the actions of the PCR unit would seem to be appropriate. It would seem reasonably clear that the matter might have resulted in a personal altercation between the prospective tenant and the landlord, or perhaps in a small claims court case. Here the matter was speedily resolved, thus avoiding possible official police involvement.

Handling of Citizen Complaints • Citizen complaints about members of the department should not be bypassed by the PCR unit. Rather, the complainant should be directed to an appropriate source within the department (either the chief or his designated representative) whose task it should be to investigate and resolve such isues. In this particular instance, as with all other service requests, the complainant should be treated with both courtesy and respect. It is most important that the complainant feel that he or she has been directed to a source of assistance rather than merely shuffled off. At the same time, the PCR unit should maintain a neutral stance in the matter.

• THE UNIT'S RESPONSIBILITIES WITHIN THE DEPARTMENT

A confusion of roles between line officer and PCR officer should be avoided at all costs. The line officer who attempts to turn over a social service problem to the PCR unit should be instructed firmly and clearly about the basic procedures in making a direct initial referral of a client to a social service agency. A successful PCR program involves the building of a sense of community responsibility in every patrol officer.

If the line officer cannot be allowed to slough off his responsibilities, the PCR unit must not be allowed by the chief administrator to develop into "just another program": just another excuse for a specialized unit to perpetuate or extend its influence in the department beyond its original mandate. An example of this danger was related by one midwestern police officer who reported a neighborhood disturbance incident to headquarters only to be told, "Don't worry about that. We have a PCR unit. They'll handle it." (Related during a seminar discussion by an in-service student.)

At its best, a PCR unit should provide practical information and counsel to the patrolman as he deals with his daily routine. Information should include specific details of particular social problems facing specific groups of individuals within the officer's patrol area. This type of process should involve an exchange of views, opinions, and strategies between line and PCR personnel about how a particular situation may best be handled. It is during this type of dialog *within* the department that the PCR unit fulfills its most important function: that of providing line personnel with an opportunity to express freely the frustrations and other emotions brought about by the everyday gaff of being a line police officer.

While many large police departments such as in Los Angeles and New York City have begun to employ full time psychologists on their staffs for a variety of functions, the smaller department cannot, for obvious reasons of economy and availability of personnel, readily obtain such assistance. While there has been much discussion of the policeman as a mental health agent, as a paraprofessional within the allied health services, most of the literature has concentrated on the officer's possible helping role to his civilian clients (Kowalewski, 1975). The PCR officer, on the other hand, has a special opportunity to assist fellow officers in overcoming the extreme stress of such events as a death notification, suicides, or psychiatric emergencies, as well as numerous other events which are no less stressful for the police officer than for the ordinary citizen. This does not mean that a PCR officer needs to be a fully trained mental health professional. What it does suggest is the need for such officers to be able to perceive the signs of extreme stress among their fellows and to play an appropriate helping role.

The following report, though written by a fictional psychiatrist, points out the urgency of this function:

> In an unsolicited opinion by this examiner to the police department, may I humbly and respectfully suggest that a careful assay be made of procedures that are presently being used to assist officers who suffer severe physical or emotional trauma. It is unfortunate that this man was not given an opportunity for psychologically working through his fear, shame, guilt, desperation, and panic, occasioned by the event [the shooting of his partner]. In my opinion, this man's emotional equilibrium could have been much more stable if immediate attention and opportunity had been given to him for psychological assistance. Perhaps all he needed at that time was some cathartic ventilation and perhaps also some restoration of his self-confidence. To assume that a man can just resume a normal way of life after such an overwhelming episode is asking too much of most of us. I do not know of the arrangement which the police department has for psychological assistance, but I urge that very careful consideration be given for the *prevention* of mental and emotional disturbances arising from traumata in the line of duty. (Wambaugh, 1973, pp. 370-371) [1]

• SELECTION OF MEMBERS FOR THE PCR UNIT

Selection of members for the PCR unit should be undertaken with considerable care. The unit should not be seen as a dumping ground for the officer who is ineffective in other assignments or, at the other extreme, who is viewed as a "nice guy" looking for a snug haven to finish out his police career. In short, the practice of selecting "somebody's

---

[1] Excerpted from *The Onion Field* by Joseph Wambaugh. Copyright © 1973 by Joseph Wambaugh. Used with the permission of Delacorte Press.

cousin" or a member of a particular ethnic group in the community is inappropriate for the goals and objectives of a PCR unit.

Members should be selected from volunteers. It should be clearly understood that the task involves considerable demands upon the individual officer including a willingness and capability to work closely and effectively with other unit members as a total team. Broomfield (1974) comments that the members of the Dayton, Ohio, conflict management team "were selected on the basis of their ability to work competently without close supervision, their sensitivity and adaptability to change, and their commitment to change through rational means." (p. 19)

The commander of the unit should be an individual who enjoys both the confidence and genuine support of the chief of police and board of civilian commissioners. As indicated earlier, such an individual should be assured of unlimited access to the chief and appropriate command officers to discuss pressing problems in full and frank terms. Considering the traditional quasi-military organization of police departments, it would seem appropriate that the unit commander should be a commissioned officer in the department. Klyman (1974) notes that at present, educational qualifications have not been stressed by departments in appointing PCR unit commanders.

While college education or academic training *per se* is highly desirable, the thrust of the federal government's equal employment opportunity programs has been to encourage recognition of those individuals who are able to perform a task not based on paper qualifications alone but on special skills and experience which allow the individual to carry out the functions of the particular job. The concept of equal opportunity is most appropriate when considering selection of candidates for unit leadership and membership.

Because the unit must be attuned to various trends in the total community, the unit commander might well be the individual who has not secured an advanced education but who possesses a large degree of what most of us might call "street smarts" or common sense. The individual who has a consistent record of handling difficult, sensitive situations, of demonstrating a capacity for personal growth and the ability to accept change, should also be considered for unit leadership, even though he may not possess certain formal educational attainments.

Before the unit begins operations there should be a considerable period of in-service training and planning by unit members with administrators. Again, because many of the goals we have outlined for a PCR unit involve considerable skill in the practical applications of the behavioral sciences, all unit members should take part in initial or refresher courses in this area.

It would be helpful if some members of the PCR unit had com-

pleted a college education with a specialization in the behavioral sciences. This would be in keeping with the recommendations of the Task
Force on Police (1973) which has established as a standard that

> every police agency should, no later than 1982, require as a condition
> of initial employment the completion of at least four years of education
> (120 semester units) or a baccalaureate degree at an accredited college
> or university. (p. 369)

Following the Dayton example, those departments that are large
enough should attempt to incorporate a mixture of uniformed and civilian
personnel in their unit. While the presence of civilians in departments
is often the subject of resistance, there are increasing instances throughout the country of effective cooperation between uniformed and civilian
"professionals."

As Broomfield (1974) suggests, the presence of civilians in the
unit underscores the concept of genuine police-community interaction.
Secondly, civilians will bring to the PCR unit a different perspective
and often a different set of skills than found among the uniformed force.
The key component is finding a combination of uniformed and civilian
personnel who share the common objectives of total community service
and commitment to change.

• GUIDES TO SUCCESS:
GOALS AND SUPPORT

In addition to training there should be clear agreement between
police administrators and unit members about the precise goals for the
unit. These goals should not be presented to the unit members by executive directive but should be the result of a careful planning period
between administrators and unit members. Again it would be wise to
provide for some degree of input from other department members in
the discussions. Line and middle management personnel who have been
brought into the initial discussions concerning the advisability of form-
ing a PCR team should again be called upon to explore their concepts
of what unit objectives should be.

The key ingredient for success of a unit, in the final analysis, will
rest with the chief executive officer of the department. His clear, un-
wavering commitment to the concept of a PCR unit or the appointment
of an individual PCR officer should be made known and underscored
to all members of the department. This commitment should include a
willingness to allow the PCR unit to function for a reasonable period of

time in order to prove its effectiveness. It should also include an un-equivocal support of stated unit goals.

Without this type of administrative commitment and clear direction by the administrator, the chances of unit success are sharply reduced. Once the unit has begun operations, the administrator should make it a point to meet with the total team on a regular, systematic basis, underscoring his support for the PCR operation. The chief should inform new recruit classes of his support for the unit, its purpose, and the role it can play in enhancing their ability to function on the job.

Administrative support for the unit should also be made clear to members of the general public. Again, goals and objectives should emphasize the unit's total community service function. Additional support should be drawn from individual citizens who took part in the planning discussions which led to the formation of the unit.

In short, unit members should be selected on the basis of commitment, relevant training and experience, and willingness to serve as community change agents. Goals and objectives should be clearly defined and endorsed beyond the "lip service" stage by key members of the police department and the civilian community.

Evaluation • A review of the literature indicates that while there is an abundance of material describing a wide variety of PCR projects and programs, there has been comparatively little done in the area of critical, systematic evaluation of PCR units.

It is vital, then, when unit goals are being established that objectives be devised and stated with the awareness that they must be capable of evaluation. Therefore, if one of the stated priorities is an increase in continuous, genuine communication between police and citizens, program success cannot be demonstrated in quantitative terms such as numbers of individuals contacted, services performed, or meetings generated. Rather, the task of the PCR commander should be to demonstrate clearly and systematically that citizens have had an increasingly vital role in shaping departmental policies and programs.

There can be little question that sophisticated evaluation, particularly for smaller departments, is a difficult process to undertake. It is often a seemingly impossible task to measure and demonstrate such subtle things as the change of attitude between officers and citizens. Nonetheless, in order for a PCR unit to truly justify its existence, an attempt must be made to examine the specific results of unit activity.

For example, if this unit generated x number of contact hours with school children through formal classroom presentations or meetings, has there been any definable change in the attitude of youngsters toward police, law enforcement, or the total criminal justice system? Such changes or lack of changes are measurable using scientifically constructed questionnaires which deal with specific attitudes. These measures also could be applied to youth or other groups with whom the PCR unit has worked. It is important that such studies be carried out well after the series of contacts has occurred if real change is to demonstrated.

If the unit has been coordinating social services with community service agencies, what is the result of these consultations? Have unit members been attending such coordinating meetings as passive bystanders or can they demonstrate they have in fact played a specific leadership role in helping develop new delivery systems of community social services that serve both police and total community needs?

If the unit has been involved in the coordination of referrals or follow-up on referrals to social agencies, what has been the result of such interraction with the other agencies? Have the citizens referred been better served? Has the police relationship with these agencies been clarified and strengthened on a day-to-day operating basis? This answer can be determined by taking a sample of such referrals and seeing how the PCR unit went about the process of closing police involvement in the matter.

PCR unit participation in recruitment efforts should be measured in something more than the number of recruitment posters handed out, advertisements placed, and general meetings held. A successful, good faith recruiting effort should indicate to an outside evaluator that unit members have been successful in identifying promising minority and female candidates and have encouraged them to apply for openings on the force.

In order for the effectiveness of a PCR unit to be objectively evaluated, it is essential that records of unit tasks and outreach efforts be maintained in such a way that they can be evaluated by an independent outside group such as a consulting firm. What is called for, simply, is the development of a research component in every PCR unit that explains departmental activities in clear, precise terms that may be easily understood and interpreted by the public and lay police commission board members.

Some Hard Questions • There are three main components of a suggested research design to test the effectiveness of the PCR unit. First of all, what is the quality of the unit's organization in terms of goal definition, general administration, record keeping, and periodic internal auditing? Secondly, what changes have occurred of a positive nature in the client group?

In this case our clients are ordinary citizens in the community. Questions that might be asked in this evaluation category are: are the citizens aware of the existence of the PCR unit? Are the unit's goals and objectives clearly understood? How have these goals been conveyed to the public? What type of citizen participation has been involved in the planning and execution of unit goals? The third and most important component would be evidence of measurable change in citizens' attitudes toward the police since the start of the PCR program. A variety of yardsticks might be used to determine this: an increase in reporting of acts of victimization; a lowering of police injuries while intervening in certain types of crisis situations; and a measurable degree of overall public support for the police in terms of a public understanding of total departmental goals.

Another basic series of questions that should be asked concerns the impact of the PCR unit on staff members. How does the staff view their role with the unit? Do they see their jobs as performing a meaningful departmental function? Has personal growth taken place among unit personnel? Do they see policing in its broader aspects?

Finally, the unit should be evaluated in terms of its impact beyond the department. Specifically, how has this particular unit contributed to the functioning of the overall criminal justice system in that particular city? Do other sub-sections of the total criminal justice system work more effectively with the police? Do all members of the department understand the need to lend their cooperation to these agencies, and are they equipped with specific training and information to help them go about this process? Perhaps most important, has the PCR unit strengthened ties between private and public helping agencies and other criminal justice agencies so that the total criminal justice system in the community is functioning in a manner that truly serves the interests of both clients and practitioners?

All these questions should be examined carefully in order to determine to some reasonable degree whether or not a police-community relations unit is really fulfilling its objectives. If not, part of the chief executive's responsibility should be to move quickly and effectively either to revamp the unit or to merge its activities with other components of the police operation.

In an era where citizens have become increasingly skeptical about the quality and direction of governmental services it is most important that the police-community relations unit not be started as a token effort or be allowed to slip into such a posture. Any PCR unit, in the final analysis, draws its strength from the credibility and confidence it *creates* among rank and file officers and citizens alike.

6

Present and Future Police Behavior

As Meier indicates in Chapter 7, police administrators as well as line officers have begun to recognize the need to develop a further understanding of basic human behavior in order to carry out effective policing.

This awareness includes the realization that officers should be aware of the impact of their own specific behaviors, as well as how they are perceived by others if they are to avoid situations which at the least may annoy citizens and at the worst may cause confrontations resulting in death or injury to the officer.

Community hostility has further implications for police. Hostile attitudes toward the police may affect the type and number of recruits for police positions. Able people generally seek occupations which have the respect and support of family and friends. If this support is missing, or if a hostile attitude prevails, surely an able young candidate will seek employment in other fields.

Community hostility presents further problems for the police. If community members are fearful of the police or feel that police will not help them, then citizens will not report crime or seek assistance from the police. Community support in crime reduction and crime prevention is absolutely necessary if police are to achieve their law enforcement goals.

Reiss (1971) indicated the necessity for police to rely on the support of the community for successful police work. He indicated that approximately 43 percent of requests for police service with regard to a felony crime took place in an enclosed private place, within a dwelling. This 43 percent represented a majority of the amount of requests for police service in this area. Thus, the police were forced to, in the majority of cases, rely on the public in order to deal with felony crimes, and, we might add, other types of incidents as well. For a further discussion of this, along with exact statistics, see Chapter 9.

Further implications revolve around the political realities of policing a democratic society. When police present budgets to local governmental authorities or when they request more men, better pay, and newer, more advanced equipment—if there is hostility toward the police, or misunderstanding and confusion concerning their function in the community, then moves to upgrade personnel and supporting services may be stymied.

Morale is yet another part of the picture. Community hostility can make the line officer less than enthusiastic about his job. Apathy or negativism may show up in two ways. First, the police officer may simply not do his job. "Sleeping" on the job for the line officer may not be an uncommon experience. Secondly, the line officer may tend to overreact to certain situations if he feels that the community is hostile toward the work that he does. He may decide to bring in reinforcements when it is uncalled for with possible dangerous effects. The riots of the 1960s stand in testimony to this fact.

This chapter is an attempt to analyze current police practices. Case materials will be presented in order to point out some typical police behaviors which are deemed inappropriate. Our purpose is not to be unduly critical of police functioning, but rather to "role play on paper" in order that we may clearly designate some current ways of handling situations in which the police could improve their image. For a further discussion of these and other similar cases see Siegal & Federman (1963).

- ## CASE STUDIES

Case One: Suspicious Persons

Officers Smith and Jones were riding a squad car on September 8. At approximately 7:00 P.M., they noticed five black persons in front of an apartment house. They looked suspicious—they were clothed in what might be described as self-styled religious robes. Although the men were only standing on the street, the police officers decided to ask them to explain why there were there. The spokesman for the group explained that they were members of _____ (a small religious sect), and were waiting for two "sisters" who had gone into the apartment house to solicit money for the church. The officers decided to wait for the two "sisters" to come out.

At this time, a third police officer approached and asked what was going on. While once again explaining their situation to the new officer, the spokesman for the group became visibly nervous. He explained that residents were only visited with an appointment and that no door-to-door soliciting was going on.

The police officers doubted that these men were solely involved in religious activities. About fifteen minutes passed and the two "sisters" did not come out of the house. Officer Jones became impatient and told the leader of the group, "I don't care what your purpose is. You're not supposed to solicit. If you were legitimate religious solicitors you would know that you would have to have the okay before you solicit. I think we'll take you all in."

By this time a sizable crowd (comprised mostly of blacks from the neighborhood) had gathered. Two of the officers tried to break up the crowd by telling them to "move along" and to "stand back." Several members of the crowd accused the police officers of having no respect for "men of the cloth." They also made remarks to the effect that the police were always picking on black people for no reason at all. At first, only one or two members of the crowd made comments, but slowly more and more people became involved.

Discussion • What happened, or better still what could have happened? Did the police officers show concern for public image and act as professionals? Were they able to defuse a potentially dangerous situation? Why did Officers Smith and Jones stop their patrol car in the first place? What was their motivation?

To the crowd, the police officers showed little tolerance for the religious beliefs of the five men. Nor were they concerned about how their behavior could affect the members of the crowd. Were they aware of the values of the people? Were they sensitive to the cultures of minority groups? Did the officers act in a professional and ethical manner, or did they appear as the hostile white enemy in the black man's camp? How did the officers' behavior affect sound police-community relations? Do you think that the five men and the members of the crowd now trust the police?

What specific things could the officers have done in this situation in order to promote a good image with the community? They could have done many different things. If their suspicions were legitimately raised by the five men, what should they have done in order to have avoided the crowd incident? First, they could have behaved in a manner to not arouse any antagonism within the crowd. Second, they should have determined the hostility of the crowd. And if there was an offense on the part of the five men (this has not been determined), perhaps it was not serious enough to create a confrontation which could have produced potential injury to both the police and the members of the crowd.

The police before deciding what action to take should have taken into consideration that some people are not aware that they have violated a law. They could and should have quietly and clearly explained the law to the five men, and then proceeded from there.

Case Two: A Problem with Prejudice

Manuel Rondez, age 26, a Puerto Rican living in this country for the past 3 years, was driving from his home to his job as a construction worker. At 6:30 A.M. he was driving on Washington Street, which is in a ghetto neighborhood predominated by blacks. He noticed two white men walking along the street. They were staggering and leaning against each other.

As Rondez approached the corner, he stopped for a red light. While waiting for the light to change, he heard the two men singing and screaming at the top of their lungs. Rondez stared at the two men. One of the men in the street noticed that Rondez was watching them and yelled, "What's the matter, Spic? Don't you like it?"

Rondez, turning to watch the light turn green, realized that the men were approaching his car. He didn't have time to roll up his windows so he locked the left door. One of the men practically leaped through the window and started to swing at him. Rondez was trying to push the man out of the car when the attacker yelled, "This Spic put his hand in my face. I won't let no Spic put his hand in my face." With this, he became more violent, and continued to swing and punch Rondez. Rondez moved out of the driver's seat to the opposite side of the car. The other man and a third party (who had subsequently joined these two) opened the right door, which was not locked, and dragged Rondez out of the car.

As Rondez was being dragged from his car, he reached down to the floor where he kept various tools and picked up a pipe; he warned the three men to keep away from him. They charged at him and a fight ensued.

Rondez yelled to the crowd which had formed, "Help me! Don't let them kill me—they're drunk." No one came from the crowd which was primarily black. Rondez finally managed to break loose and rolled on top of one of the men. While pinning the man to the ground, Rondez reached into his pocket, pulled out a knife, and put it to the attacker's throat. Rondez called to the other two, "If you don't stop fighting me, I'm going to slit his throat." Shortly, Rondez noticed a police officer, gun in hand, breaking through the crowd.

As the policeman approached the fight, one of the bystanders stopped him and said, "These men are drunk. I saw them attack him." The police officer ignored the man and separated the two fighting. The officer then took the knife from Rondez. The man who was pinned to the ground by Rondez jumped to his feet and started to swing at Rondez. The police officer pushed him aside saying, "Come on, buddy. Take it easy." The man then began to swing at the officer, yelling, "Get your hands off me! I'm going to kill that Spic."

At the same time, two other police officers, who had just arrived, jumped on the man and handcuffed him. The first officer grabbed Rondez and said to the other man, "Don't worry about this guy. We'll take care of him."

At this point, Rondez blurted out several sentences in Spanish. The police officer replied, "Speak English! Speak English!" Rondez belligerently replied, "Sure go on—blame it on me. It's all my fault. You cops don't give us people a break." With this, he spat on the officer. The officer then punched Rondez in the face and handcuffed him.

Discussion • Do you think that Rondez, as a member of a minority group, felt abused and discriminated against by the police officers? What should the officers have done? Did the police officers act in a professional manner, carefully considering what implications their actions could have toward public relations?

There are several things that the police officers should have done in this situation. To begin with, the police should always attempt to control the situation or at least to mask their own prejudices in enforcing the law. Also, the police officers should have gathered the facts from the people concerned at the scene of the incident before making decisions regarding arrest. In this case, the police officers made a wrong judgment about whom they should arrest and deliberately provoked Rondez into abusing an officer. The quick, unthinking actions on the part of the police showed their total lack of concern for public respect and support so vital to policing. All that was required of the officers was to break up the fight, find out what happened and why, and then take the necessary action. In other words, what was required of the police was a *professional, controlled* response.

Case Three

Case three is presented as a model of professional, humane police service. No discussion or commentary follows as we feel that the story speaks for itself.

At 10:00 P.M. on January 20, Patrolman Parker, walking his beat in a neighborhood characterized by its slums, high-density housing, low rentals, and numerous bars, noticed a man staggering along the street. It was a cold, windy night and the streets were covered with ice as a result of a newly fallen snow. Parker suspected that the man was drunk. He politely approached the man and asked, "Are you feeling all right?" The man replied, "Go peddle your marbles someplace else." Parker, who could smell liquor on the man's breath, ignored this comment and told the drunk to go home because he could be "rolled" in his present condition. The officer reached out to grab hold of the man's arm, as the drunk swayed from side to side. The drunk told him, "Get your hands off me." Parker, once again ignoring this comment, said "Come on, go home and go to bed." He watched as the drunk walked away.

• THE POLICE CULTURE

We have been discussing the effects and models of poor police-community relations. Before moving on to other areas of police behavior, let us examine how the police are alienated from the total community. The police culture, as Fortier (1972) and others have termed it, is largely responsible for the alienation of police from the mainstream of community life.

What is the police culture? What is culture? Generally culture is defined as any patterned set of behaviors associated with a particular group. There are several patterned sets of behavior associated with the police group. The first type of behavior may be called, for the lack of a better word, cynicism. Many authors have written about police cynicism and Niederhoffer (1967) has devoted an entire book to the subject.

And yet, what does cynicism mean? The cynic is one who is wholly distrustful of human nature and motivation. He believes that most people are spurred on only by their own self-interest. There is that key quality of trust missing from the cynic's philosophy of life. Cynicism, it should be noted, is a learned behavioral response. Individuals are not born cynical. With the case of the police, it is easily seen how they become cynical. As Fortier (1972) suggests, the policeman sees many of the vagaries of human existence:

He sees adultery, incest, homosexuality, bestiality, and other examples of the "games people play," on a daily basis. In addition, he is exposed to the "normal" human vagaries such as stealing, personal crime against other persons, and the tragic, needless accidents with their innocent victims. (p. 33)

This, we suggest, may lead some police officers to become cynical about the human experience. Their cynicism which is reinforced daily as they interact with the community on the street and with their fellow officers has a profound effect on the way in which the police deal with citizen encounters. The end result may be poor police-community relations with all the implications discussed earlier.

Niederhoffer (1967) notes: "It is possible to describe two types of police cynicism. One is directed against life, the world and people in general; the other is aimed at the police system itself" (p. 100). Thus, Niederhoffer contends that cynicism is a learned process that may be seen on a continuum, stemming from commitment on the part of the new recruit to the police goals and organization, to a frustration and disenchantment with the organization and goals of the police, ending finally in cynicism aimed both at society and the police organization itself.

A second aspect of the so-called police culture is isolationism. This phenomenon may be a direct result of cynicism. If a police officer mistrusts the community, he may find himself drifting away from community members, both in an occupational and in a social sense. The police officer begins to distinguish between "we" and "they": "we," the police, and "they," the civilians.

Perhaps because of the nature of the job, certainly because of the hours they keep and the uniforms they wear, police are almost automatically isolated from the rest of the community. Stark (1972) comments that the police are "not only different from most of the rest of us in terms of their conceptions about the world, but like nuns and hippies they have a distinctive garb which sets them apart" (p. 89).

Sociologist Jerome Skolnick (1966), addressing himself to the problem of isolation, states that the two-role variables of danger and authority tend to separate the policeman from society.

The element of danger seems to make the policeman especially attentive to signs indicating a potential for violence and lawbreaking. As a result, the policeman is generally a "suspicious" person. Furthermore, the character of the policeman's work makes him less desirable as a friend, since the norms of friendship implicate others in his work. Accordingly, the element of danger isolates a policeman socially from that segment of the citizenry which he regards as symbolically dangerous and also from the conventional citizenry with whom he identifies.

The element of authority reinforces the element of danger in isolating the policeman. Typically, the policeman is required to enforce laws representing puritanical morality, such as those prohibiting drunkenness, and also laws regulating the flow of public activity, such as traffic laws. In those situations the policeman directs the citizenry, whose typical response denies recognition to his authority, and stresses his obligation to respond to danger. (p. 44) [1]

Directly related to isolationism is the notion of group coalescence. Policemen work together, fight adversaries together, socialize together, and protect each other. Because he is isolated from the community, the police officer must turn to someone for support and friendship, and that someone usually turns out to be his fellow officer. After all, who understands a cop better than another cop? The police now have become a group, a culture with their own norms and values. Fortier (1972) writes:

The (new) policeman soon learns that it is far easier to "get along" with other policemen, and that only other policemen understand him and can relate to his personal feelings. The new officer learns that to violate the "trust" of his fellow officers is paramount to a violation of any formalized rules and regulations. (p. 34)

Westley (1970) addresses himself to this concept of group support and cohesiveness by examining and questioning whether or not a patrolman would be willing to testify against other policemen for certain official misconducts.

Table 6.1   Proportion of Policemen Willing to Testify Against Other Policemen

Response	Frequency	Percentage
Would not testify	10	77
Would testify	3	23
Total	13 *	100

* Two men refused to answer the question.

Reprinted from: William A. Westley. *Violence and the Police.* Cambridge, Mass.: The MIT Press, 1970, p. 114.

---

[1] From *Justice Without Trial* by J. Skolnick. New York: Wiley, 1966. Copyright 1966. Reprinted by permission of John Wiley & Sons, Inc.

Simple analysis indicates that 77 percent of the polled police officers would be unwilling to testify against their "brother" police officers. This would certainly seem to indicate a substantial amount of group coalition and/or cohesiveness at least in this particular study.

McNamara (1967) further examining this notion of police group cohesiveness presents the following data:

Table 6.2   Perceived Cohesiveness among Patrolmen (in Percent)

Item	Group	No Answer	Strongly Agree	Agree	Un-certain	Dis-agree	Strongly Dis-agree
A	T_1	0	29	43	14	13	1
	T_2	1	25	47	11	14	2
	T_3	0	20	49	11	17	3
	T_4	0	17	52	6	20	5
B	T_1	1	42	40	8	8	1
	T_2	0	57	31	4	8	6
	T_3	1	61	26	4	7	1
	T_4	1	47	34	5	12	1
C	T_1	1	54	42	2	1	0
	T_2	5	58	34	2	1	0
	T_3	0	69	28	1	0	2
	T_4	0	64	33	2	0	1
D	T_1	0	4	20	26	39	11
	T_2	0	2	20	17	43	18
	T_3	0	3	19	11	46	21
	T_4	0	2	28	16	42	12

Source: John H. McNamara. "Uncertainties in Police Work: The Relevance of Police Recruits' Background and Training" in Bordua, David. *The Police: Six Sociological Essays.* New York: Wiley, 1967, p. 246.

The degree of perceived cohesiveness among patrolmen at the beginning of their training, as well as at other intervals early in their career, tends to be high due to the strong agreement that patrolmen constitute a "brotherhood" (item A) and that assistance from other patrolmen is not a rare commodity (items B and C). They further concur with one another in disagreeing that a significant number of patrolmen will avoid helping other patrolmen (item D). (p. 246)

Thus, the police have created their own culture. Sometimes it acts as a "counterculture" and becomes detrimental to the good of the total community. Such a culture rejects values of other community members (and sometimes legal values) and thus serves as one of the single most destructive elements in fostering good police-community relations.

What can be done to break this cycle of isolation and cynicism that separates the police from the total community? What can the police administrator do to begin to break down the counterculture? Two changes are immediately apparent. The first deals with recruitment. The police need to recruit capable, well qualified young men and women in order to create a professional force capable of delivering services to the community. No longer should the police accept the average candidate. Entrance requirements for new police officers should include some college work, and an eventual college degree of some kind.[2] The major national commissions including the President's Commission on Law Enforcement and the Administration of Justice and the National Advisory Commission on Criminal Justice Standards and Goals have recommended that higher education for police is necessary for a career in law enforcement.

> A 1972 study of the New York Police, "Police Background Characteristics and Performance," revealed that men with at least 1 year of college were very good performers and had fewer civilian complaints than the average. The men who had college degrees demonstrated even better on-the-job performance; they had a low incidence of all types of misconduct—except harassment, on which they were average—and took less sick leave. Generally speaking, the older, better educated officer received fewer civilian complaints than the younger, less educated officer. (National Advisory Commission on Criminal Justice Standards and Goals, *Police* (1973), p. 370)

Lateral entry or employment of a candidate by a police department who has not occupied a lower rank in the department should be made available. For example, a department might wish to fill a vacancy at the sergeant's level by hiring a candidate who had not previously served with the department as a patrolman but who had served as a sergeant with another police department. Another possibility would be employing an

---

[2] The Dallas, Texas Police Department, among others, requires at least one year of college preparation before joining the force. For a further discussion of this, see Saunders (1970); and National Advisory Commission on Criminal Justice Standards and Goals, *Police* (1973).

individual who had superior educational attainment and/or other qualifications at a higher entry rank than traditional practices would call for.

Lateral entry, or the movement into an organizational position based on qualifications without first occupying a lower position, should be made available to the properly qualified candidate. For example, it is reasonable to suggest that one could occupy the role of police administrator without ever having been a line officer, provided that the individual is properly qualified. It is not necessary, nor is it a common occurrence in business, for the manufacturing company president to have started out operating machines that produce his product in order to properly manage his company. So it is true for the police—from an organizational and management point of view, the police administrator need not have been a line officer first in order to properly manage the department or any of the levels of it.

It is a vital necessity that the police be able to recruit those individuals who possess entry level professional education in order that the police become the type of organization needed for effective delivery of social services, crime prevention and apprehension, and order maintenance. We must elevate the position of policeman to that of a professional; one of the most widely recognized ways of achieving this is through education. Just as psychiatrists, psychologists, social workers and other helpers are required to have attained a certain level of professional college training, so should the police.

The second change needed that is immediately apparent is in the area of police training. Not only do the police need a general college education, but they also need specific training in actual police functions. Training should emphasize psychology, sociology, law, crisis intervention, and police technology as well as the traditional weapons training, first aid, and physical fitness.

• POSITIVE
POLICE WORK

The police are no longer able to effect the so-called "cosmetic" changes in order to improve relations with the community. The police must look to their own "house" for solutions to the many problems that they face. By altering in some cases, and by adding in other cases, the police can improve on the total service impact by developing and enhancing the preparation and the role of the line officer in particular.

There are a variety of means by which the police can convey their total service mission to the community. For example, consider the news media. Police activities, and often policemen themselves, have long occupied a spotlight position with both radio and television. This is particularly true in the case of television. Few would dispute the fact that television has had a great impact on modern American society. A typical broadcast might show police officers arresting, controlling, and otherwise enforcing the law. This may have negative consequences for the police, as sociologist Edwin Schur (1969) has pointed out. Policemen are shown, particularly to ghetto area residents and other minorities as forces—oppressive forces, of the ruling political powers. This may cause the community to become unnecessarily fearful of police action. The police have little power over the content of media news presentations in particular. To partially counteract the negative feelings concerning the police that may be conveyed by the media, the police ought to begin what in effect would be an advertising campaign.

The police, as politicians have done, should take advantage of television's impact and present "spots" showing the vast number of positive activities that they perform daily. The police could use the media to bolster their image in the community in much the same way political candidates do at election time. It might be very surprising indeed to find community members "voting" in favor of their police. Such activities could also show citizens that the police are interested in their well-being, and serve as an opportunity for the police to communicate a variety of facts and information, on a wholesale basis, to the public.

Berkley (1969) commenting on police behavior indicates that a positive approach to police work is generally called for. The police need to emphasize the many positive aspects and elements of their role. Unfortunately, the community rarely hears, or sees for that matter, the many, many "good" things that police officers do; rather, we are constantly reminded of the daily arrests, shootouts, and other forms of social control that the police participate in. Berkley reports of the instructions given to the Metropolitan police of London in 1820:

> . . . every member of the force must remember that it is his duty to protect and help members of the public, no less than to bring offenders to justice (because) the approval and cooperation of the public (weigh heavily in the performance of their peace-keeping functions). (p. 89)

And as First Assistant Olaf Ephraimsson of the Swedish police said:

> Police service is full of work which requires one to be repressive and to interfere with the citizen's life in various unpleasant ways. These duties are necessary and will always be a part of our work. But, in the eyes of the public and in the eyes of the individual policeman, this makes us somewhat onesided . . . if we now through crime prevention can

counter balance the repressive element, then I believe our whole profession will profit considerably. (pp. 89-90)

Thus, the police need to stress their involvement with more positive things.
Crime prevention activities certainly occupy a large amount of the positive police work. Included here are police work with juveniles and other
community groups, and with other community agencies such as schools
and mental health clinics.

There exists in most police departments today another source of potential change. This source is the police union or professional association.
One might ask what the police union has to do with police-community
relations? In our opinion, the police union could have a significant effect
on the relationship that the police have with the community.

At the present time, most police associations are concerned with
the day-to-day functioning of the department from the employees' stand-
point. They are primarily concerned that the policemen and others receive a "fair shake" from the department. And yet, why couldn't the police
union act in the same manner as the American Bar Association (ABA),
or in some cases, as the American Medical Association (AMA)? Both of
these national professional associations include such groups as standing
committees which regulate professional education and training. Why
couldn't the local police associations do the same thing? The answer is
they could and should.

By utilizing the police association, the police could improve education and training standards for officers, lobby in the necessary legislatures,
and in general help change or professionalize the police.

What is needed within the present police association is a dedication
to the general improvement of the police and a commitment to better
police-community relations. The police union must turn its focus from
protecting the interests of the individual officer to a total community
centered orientation. This is not to suggest that the police union should
forget about safeguarding its own department members, but rather, to
state that its primary emphasis should shift toward general improvements
in police functioning.

Individual police officers can also effect changes which will help to
bring about better police-community relations. Police need to involve
themselves in all aspects of life in their communities. They must conceive
of themselves as members of the community, instead of thinking in terms
of the traditional "we-they" dichotomy. They must work to become an
integral part of life in the community, rather than separate from it.

In summary, we have attempted to look at police behavior as it
presently exists with the hope of presenting some reasonable alternatives.
We have indicated that new standards in recruitment, training, and edu-

cation are necessary—vitally necessary—for sound police-community relations. We have also examined some case situations in which police may frequently find themselves and have presented some alternative ways of handling them. And we have explored the better use of both the media and the police association. By recognizing and acting upon these alternatives, the police will be able to build better relationships with the community, and thus be more effective in policing.

❨ 7 ❩

Bridging the Gap: A Psychologist's View of the Problem*

* Written by Robert D. Meier, Division of Criminal Justice, University of New Haven, West Haven, Conn. Dr. Meier received his Ph.D. in Counseling Psychology from Columbia University in 1972.

Law enforcement officials and personnel throughout America are faced with tremendous, almost insurmountable problems of crime and disorder in their communities. Psychology, the science of behavior, is by its very nature faced with a great challenge to respond to the situation. Too often, however, a response to the challenge is thwarted by ineffective interaction between practicing police and behavioral scientists.

Robert di Grazia, the Boston Police Commissioner, has called attention to this unfortunate state of affairs.

> As with other academicians, social scientists have begun to view the operation of the criminal justice system as an object for serious study—and often for critical comment. Criminal justice practitioners, especially the police, have tended to look with suspicion at those interested social scientists, believing that they were generally overly liberal, unfairly critical, and insensitive to the realities facing those working in the system. Indeed few social scientists have been able to effectively communicate with criminal justice practitioners, and few criminal justice practitioners have been able or willing to take advantage of social science theory in their practice. A failure of communications has been an important deterrent to integration of the two disciplines. (Parker & Meier, 1975, p. xix)

There are many similarities between the two disciplines that suggest the advantages of a more open sharing of ideas and methods. Farmer and Kowalewski have pointed out in other sections of this volume that much, perhaps even most, of the work of the law enforcement officer involves service activities and responsibilities. The police officer must face and attempt to defuse hostile, often violent, conflicts. He must intervene directly in situations involving extremely deviant or mentally disturbed individuals. He must console the person who is despondent or in the midst of personal tragedy. He is thrust into the lives of human beings at the most critical times in their lives. To be effective the officer must have not only the psychological tools, but also adequate self-awareness, self-understanding, and the knowledge necessary to assess the behavior of others. He must be aware of the principles of human behavior in terms of relating his actions to the potential responses of others, and in terms of predicting the behavior of individuals and groups.

One would be hard pressed to find major differences between these service-related job requirements for the police officer and those demanded of the practicing psychologist or social worker. Yet, the major focus of police training is not directed at these activities as it is for the social service professional. Badalamente, Clay, Halterlein, Jackson, Moore, and Rio (1973) note that "Despite the magnitude and importance of the policeman's social role, few police agencies devote adequate time to developing the necessary traits, knowledge and other skills in police trainees. Neither do they require periods at retraining of police regulars." (p. 453)

Once it is recognized that psychological skills are necessary for effective police work, a second step is to develop efficient and productive ways to increase the communications and cooperation between social scientists and police practitioners. Several psychologists have recently attempted to close the gap between the two fields by preparing material specifically oriented to the law enforcement field, for example Bard (1969, 1970), Parker and Meier (1975), and Reiser (1972). While such efforts are important, they can be successful only if greater communication is established and adversary attitudes are diminished. The valuable exchange of ideas, methods, techniques, and concerns, and the serious evaluation of the implementation of ideas can occur only in an atmosphere of mutual respect, trust, and sharing.

Perhaps one way the conflict between social scientists and the police can be viewed is through an analysis of how each perceives the other, and whether these perceptions are accurate. In the first instance, the social scientist or psychologist is often pictured as the "egghead" who has read the books, but who has never experienced the "street." He treats "sick" people, or perhaps studies them, but is often a little strange himself as well. He likes to give advice, but hates to be wrong, and if confronted will hide behind the "Ph.D." he carries around on the end of his name.

The "cop" on the other hand, is often viewed as the symbol of authority, and sometimes authoritarianism. He may be seen as not very bright, and needing to brandish his ego with black, shiny leather, a big stick and a fast car with flashing lights and siren. He may be thought of as narrow-minded and probably conservative.

This author believes that both stereotypes are inaccurate, and have severely limited communication between two of the most critical occupational groups in our society.

Perhaps the following observations regarding both social scientists and police practitioners will suggest possible steps in closing the gap.

1 · While both of these occupational groups are of great importance in our society, neither has been highly successful in making an impact on the problem of crime and social deviance. Lack of success can lead individuals to compensate by criticizing others. Such a defense is at best ineffective. Improvement is much more likely if the two parties cooperate in their efforts.

2 · Each of the two groups does have a large body of knowledge and expertise which the other does not have—a fact which need not be threatening to either group. The psychologist or social scientist should not feel he must apologize to the police officer because he has not walked the beat, but neither should he attempt to teach correct policing. On the other hand, the police officer should not feel that he has become an expert in all phases of human behavior merely by doing his time on the street.

3 · Effective teaching and learning comes from a sharing of the knowledge specific to each field in an atmosphere which can provide an open examination of issues, productive interaction and confrontation. Zacker (1974) has referred to the need for "participant learning" when offering instruction in social intervention to police officers. In an area where so little is known, it is counterproductive for the social scientist and the law enforcement professional to debate who is right.

Hopefully, current barriers between those identified primarily with the criminal justice system and those identified with the behavioral sciences can be removed. Greater communication, respect, and cooperation is essential in establishing the social-community service model discussed earlier.

• THE ROLE OF PSYCHOLOGY
IN THE FULL SERVICE MODEL

As the fields of law enforcement and psychology begin to interact more openly and effectively, careful thought must be given to the role psychology and psychologists will play in a full service model. This writer has outlined several basic propositions or recommendations regarding the application of psychological principles to criminal justice problems, including those related to police-community relations (Parker and Meier, 1975). In actuality, these ideas are not limited to applications in criminal justice or this particular model but provide helpful guidelines in applying behavioral science principles to a wide variety of human and social interventions. Each of these ideas or propositions will be discussed here in terms of the police and their functioning in the community.

Theory Bound Approaches Tend to be Overly Restrictive • Those who apply psychological or behavioral principles frequently adhere quite rigidly to a particular theoretical point of view. Such steadfast loyalty can have a number of negative effects on the outcome of social intervention. An unnecessary amount of time and energy can be spent defending a particular approach or concept on theoretical grounds rather than on its practical merits. In addition, like any rigid position, it can seriously limit the possible options one can take to solve problems. At a time when no one theoretical position has a monopoly on the facts or the methods of successful community intervention, practitioners must search for what is effective, rather than try to fit what they do into a predetermined theoretical context. Finally, blind allegiance to a theory or theories can have the effect of further isolating the psychologist from the police practitioner. The practitioners and consumers of services in the criminal justice system can often see more clearly the weaknesses of the theory bound applications than the scientist or consultant who proposes them. Psychological principles must be meaningful and lead to effective change in the real world if they are to be accepted and utilized by those in the law enforcement profession.

Judge Bazelon (1972) emphasizes this concern by telling a story about a mother who calls the doctor for her sick son. When the doctor arrives he asks the woman about the boy's condition. "Is he having fits?" The mother answers that he is not. "That's too bad," the doctor responds, "I'm terrific on fits." Behavioral scientists may have terrific theories, but the important question is whether they are relevant to the problems faced by police in the community.

Psychological principles applied to law enforcement must begin to take a "non-school" approach. Such a recommendation is aimed not only at the psychologist who offers his expertise, but also at the law enforcement practitioner as well. It is as tempting for the law enforcement officer to adopt a particular theory by which to guide his interventions as it is for the psychologist. Avila (1972) offers some advice which all of us in the field of criminal justice should heed. "It is long past time for us to begin talking about and developing a humane psychology, and to stop wasting time and energy arguing about the differences between theoretical positions." (p. 579)

The Emphasis Should be on Techniques • If applications of the behavioral sciences to the field of law enforcement cannot be guided by theory, then by what can they be guided? London (1972) has suggested that if theory is lacking, we move from a science to a *technology,* and at this point in time such an adjustment is required. The goal of the relationship between psychology and law enforcement must be the development of effective, meaningful interventions and valid solutions, rather than an endless defense of theory.

Lazarus (1971) has carried into practice an attempt to separate techniques from theory. He states:

> As an ever-increasing number of therapeutic systems mushroom into existence, it becomes impossible to keep pace with the field. Theorists who try to integrate assumptions from divergent systems often end up embracing incompatible notions. Those who identify exclusively with one or two schools of thought often find that their devotion eventually leads to diminishing returns. But those clinicians who are willing to employ any technique that has been shown to be effective empirically, regardless of its point of origin, manage to extract the active ingredients from a vast array of different systems. (p. xii)

While Lazarus is speaking specifically about the use of techniques in the clinical practice of psychology, the practice of law enforcement has many similarities and can gain from following the same rationale. Today's police officer must face and intervene in highly complex personal and social situations. To be even minimally successful, he must incorporate into his professional repertoire tools and methods on which he can rely and which he knows are effective. The behavioral scientist and the law enforcement professional together must develop and evaluate a technology which provides the tools to permit successful intervention in human problems.

The Technology Must Stress Interpersonal Relations   •   It must be emphasized that a technology does not imply a cold, mechanistic, unfeeling attitude toward people. It does not portray them as robots to be manipulated. Using effective techniques within a full service model in no way prevents the police officer from caring about the people he serves. On the contrary, it demonstrates an even greater concern than many of the ineffective practices of the past.

Too often when stress is placed on the specific skills in the handling of interpersonal relationships, this emphasis may be viewed as a weakness or relinquishment of authority. However, true authority comes from respect and effective communication—not fear. One can be forceful, show authority and demand respect, but unless he can communicate with others adequately and honestly, his overall effectiveness as a police officer will be diminished.

The Techniques Must be Exposed to Empirical Evaluation   •   It has become obvious that empirical evaluation of the application of psychological principles is a necessary part of the intervention process. The psychologist and the practitioner must demonstrate that what they do is effective. Too often methods evolve from "expert opinions," tradition, and even personal biases, and have little relationship to the desired outcomes or goals. In law enforcement work, especially, there are certain assumptions that underlie many traditional methods, but which are rarely, if ever, demonstrated to be valid. The empirical approach, on the other hand, demands that one must deal with facts which are determined by observation and experimentation. Any belief or conclusion is accepted only after being tested by objective methods and experience. The tools or techniques developed by the behavioral scientist and police practitioner must be required to meet the test of empiricism.

Some psychologists have suggested that the precise relationship between all major variables in an intervention must be examined in the applied behavioral sciences. They believe that outcome research should attempt to answer the question "*What* treatment, by *whom* is most effective for *this* individual with that specific problem, and under which set of circumstances?" (Bergin, 1971). Application of psychology to law enforcement problems must begin to answer each part of this question as well. Too frequently, we expect to solve our criminal justice problems by attempting to apply more and more of the old unproven methods.

Empirical study and evaluation must be an active part of any social-community service model. Psychologists and police officers alike have been too reluctant to have their techniques and methods evaluated. A constructive evaluation component is an essential part of any intervention model.

The Technology Must Be Wide Ranging, Not Narrow in Scope • One misunderstanding about psychology as a discipline must be corrected before it can be sensibly viewed as a complement to the work of the police officer. Frequently people believe that psychologists are concerned only with the study and treatment of individuals with mental disorders. However, such an impression is extremely limited in regard to a discipline involved with *all* human behavior. The possible applications of psychology in a cooperative effort with the police are virtually unlimited. Police officers and psychologists can together improve effectiveness in areas such as training and selection, staff management, morale, community and public relations, supervision of personnel, organizational management, service and intervention skills, community organization and social relations, and personal adjustment on the part of officers to the stress characteristics of police work.

The Technology Must Be Public • It should be clear that the propositions and recommendations presented so far do not limit the use of behavioral science techniques to those with professional degrees in psychology. Many people including police officers practice interpersonal psychology every day. Psychological technology which leads to greater communication and understanding between human beings must not be reserved for use by a select few. Miller (1969), a former president of the American Psychological Association, has suggested that we "give psychology away" in the sense that non-psychologists be taught scientifically valid psychological principles and techniques. Police officers operating in the full service model can benefit significantly from such knowledge and skills.

This writer believes that psychology can offer much more than it has to the law enforcement profession. However, cooperation between the two areas depends on their approaching each other from the position of exchanging ideas and information, not from a position of defensiveness. It also depends on an approach which reflects the propositions discussed above. Perhaps then, these two critical fields can join in making a major and effective gain in dealing with troubled and troublesome human beings.

(8)

Crisis Intervention: A Tool for the Line Officer

As Meier pointed out in the preceding chapter, the police officer who is aware of behavioral skills is equipped with valuable tools that will increase his own effectiveness as both law enforcer and helper.

Perhaps one of the most vital areas in which officers should possess a knowledge of probable human behavior is the situation of family crises and neighborhood disputes. They are almost certain to face the problem of intervening in these situations.

The U. S. Department of Justice: FBI *Uniform Crime Reports—1973* (1974) note that during 1969-1973, 73 law enforcement officers were killed while responding to disturbance calls (p. 41). In addition, a high percentage of all assaults on police occur during officers' involvement in dealing with disturbance calls. As Meier has pointed out, the line police officer and administrator have been searching for better ways to handle these situations. The crisis intervention methods described below are not offered as an absolute formula for successful intervention. Rather they present a set of tested techniques for line officers to consider in addition to their own knowledge of human behavior.

While most studies of domestic crisis intervention have occurred in urban settings, there is growing evidence that the problem has major implications for small town departments as well. Galliher, Donavan and Adams (1975), in a study of small town police departments in Missouri, discovered that 18% of all complaints received concerned family disturbances. An additional 19% of all complaints concerned public peace disturbances (including public intoxication). This represents over a third of the requests for police service in these small towns.

Neubauer (1974), in his study of Prairie City, a midwestern community of 90,000, reports the attitude of local police toward family disturbance calls:

> For the officer answering the call, there are several difficulties. First, he has little beyond common sense upon which to rely. He is called upon to arbitrate a long-seething disagreement. His ability to arrest also is limited. If the dispute is on private property, he has limited arrest powers. In addition, the complainant (usually the wife) may not want to file charges—just quiet her husband down. When an arrest is made, the wife may become belligerent with the officer. Many police officers are killed or injured in handling husband-wife fights. (p. 130)

The Prairie City police obviously disliked handling such offenses. The official policy was to avoid making an arrest. As the chief commented: "What good does it do to arrest—you'll probably end up taking the food money for the kids to pay the fine." (p. 130)

For line officers it is not merely the sheer volume of calls nor the possibility of physical injury that makes family crises and similar disturbance calls so vexing. It is the non-routine nature of each situation which has led officers to voice their feelings of inadequacy about their ability to effectively contain and resolve such disputes.

The task of dealing frequently with highly unpredictable situations has a definite negative effect on the line officer. Kroes, Margolis, and Hurrell (1974) in a study of line officers in Cincinnati, Ohio, report that 60 of 100 officers interviewed mentioned crisis situations as a particularly bothersome stressor. The authors suggested that, in effect, the physical dangers involved in such situations "may be kept from consciousness for one's psychological well-being. After all, if an officer is continually worried about danger to life, many wouldn't maintain their sanity or their jobs for very long" (p. 148).

The implication of the importance of more effective handling of family crisis situations and related peace-disturbance service requests is clear in terms of effective community relations.

If calls are being processed by officers who are ill-trained or unsure of their abilities to manage the situation successfully, two things are likely to occur, and in fact, often do occur. Either the police are viewed as bumbling at best—or at the worst, heavy-handed intruders in a private domestic or neighborhood situation. The result is that complaints are filed against the intervening officer for alleged abuse. As stated earlier, in extreme cases police intervention results in a physical attack against the officer.

It is also clear that the high level of stress among officers dealing with such situations is counterproductive to their handling of crisis problems and reduces their efficiency in dealing with everyday police matters.

As suggested earlier, for many departments it would be highly appropriate that the PCR unit serve as the department's main response to such crisis situations. By the very nature of their selection and in-service training, PCR unit members will be equipped with the broad basic knowledge of human behavior as well as having demonstrated success in dealing with the public in extremely sensitive situations. For most departments, however, the job of the PCR unit as a direct service agency in crisis intervention situations should be of a specfically limited duration only. One of the tasks of the PCR unit should be to identify, train, and encourage a nucleus of officers on each shift to handle family disturbances and similar neighborhood disputes.

• CRISIS DEFINED

At this point it is important that we clearly understand what is involved when a person is in crisis. While there are a variety of definitions and interpretations, Caplan's (1974) comments perhaps best illustrate the situation. He observes that a crisis occurs when an individual faces a situation that is "for a time insurmountable through the utilization of customary methods of problem solving" (p. 17). Parad and Resnik (1975) suggest that a crisis is often not life threatening and has been gathering momentum over some time. "If attended to immediately, it can usually be 'dealt with' over the following 12 to 24 hours." (p. 5)

Not all crises are the result of long standing pressures. Individuals often find it impossible to deal with the sudden stress of an auto accident; the death of a partner, spouse, or child; or the experience of being involved in a natural disaster.

In the instances of long building and sudden crisis there is one central common element: the coping (problem solving) ability of the individual(s) involved has ceased to function. Immediate, truly helpful intervention is needed.

There are several key tasks to be performed by the line officer acting as crisis intervener. First, the precipitating cause of the crisis should be identified as specifically as possible. This does not mean that the officer is to attempt a full scale reconstruction of the individual's life. In short, the officer should view his task as that of a mental health, first aid agent with limited goals. As Shneidman (1973) has commented, "You need not aspire to do more." (p. 11) The job at hand is to soften the impact of the crisis and help the client begin to cope with the situation. Therefore the officer should attempt to focus the attention of the client to the here and now.

The next step for the officer is to determine what resources should be called to help the individual deal with the crisis. One should determine if there are close friends, family, or other "significant" persons whom the client wishes summoned. The officer must clearly understand the problem before he can effectively mobilize community resources.

If the client needs the assistance of other resources, the officer should be prepared to provide clear, concise, specific information about what he has observed during his intervention. It is important that the officer be most specific in the type of referral that he makes. A referral is appropriate *only* when it meets the specific needs of the individual client.

One of the major tasks of a PCR unit in overseeing crisis intervention situations is to establish links with agencies and community resources who have both the ability and the willingness to help. Their resources should be made known to all department members who engage in crisis work. Individual officers should also be encouraged to establish their own referral sources.

Simply put, the officer dealing with the distressed party should have the confidence and training to make his own referral. This requires that the officer know who the real agency helpers are: that he know key individuals in both traditional and innovative helping agencies. Frequently, the best way for him to discover this is to listen to citizens talk about which helping agencies really are interested in helping, and then to make himself known to their personnel.

Once the client has been referred for assistance by an officer, a follow-up call should be made to the agency which received the service request. This should be undertaken by the line officer who initiated the referral. This is a simple and uncomplicated process usually requiring no more than a few minutes of the officer's time. The process serves two purposes. It indicates to the client that the officer is genuinely interested in his situation, and reassures the helping agencies that police have not just dumped a client on their doorstep but are seeking to build an effective professional relationship.

• CASE STUDIES

Several brief case studies based on actual experience may help illustrate what is involved in successful crisis intervention.

Case One

On a rainy, late evening in a southern state, a black youth whom we will call Marvin suddenly experienced an auto breakdown. Using a roadside telephone he summoned his father to the scene and the two men began to repair the automobile. Due to the poor weather conditions and the lateness of the hour the father was not seen by a passing motorist and was hit and instantly killed by the other auto. Police and the usual emergency vehicles were called to the scene. As a police officer began to question Marvin about the details of the accident, he noticed that the youth was extremely upset by the tragedy and that as Marvin began to talk, he indicated a feeling of guilt for having summoned his father to what resulted in his death. The police officer quietly abandoned his role of questioner and adopted the role of helper. He put away his pad and pencil, removed his cap which served as a symbol of police authority, and carried on an extensive conversation with Marvin in a quiet, casual manner, allowing the youth to fully express his feelings about the tragedy. Finally the officer suggested that there was no reason for Marvin to remain at the scene. A passer-by who had been helpful offered to provide Marvin a ride to his home. The youth replied, "Thank you very much for helping me out, but I don't want to put you out any further. If I can, I'd rather ride home with this gentleman [the police officer]."

Case Two

A good example of an appropriate referral and follow up by an alert police department can be demonstrated by the following case: Estelle an elderly lady, arrived at the capital city welfare office and demanded that she be furnished with aid. If she was not served, she declared, she would remain in the office until provided assistance. The welfare director assumed by the woman's actions that she was emotionally disturbed. Police were summoned and the woman was quietly removed from the welfare office, presented before local court officials, and after a preliminary medical examination, committed for observation to a state mental health facility. Meanwhile the police-community relations unit had asked court officials to notify them when the woman was next presented in court because she had no immediate friends or family in the city. After the mandatory holding period had expired, the hearing judge dismissed disorderly conduct charges against Estelle and released her, finding no evidence of mental illness. The PCR unit, in the meantime, mobilized community resources. The local Human Relations Council —because the director was known to the PCR officers to be an effective helper, relatively unhampered by legal ties—was asked to locate temporary housing and to contact any possible relatives. Numerous telephone calls were exchanged between the two agencies to make sure that the case was being followed up by both agencies. An attorney who represented the woman's interest was located and he furnished an account of her financial resources. Arrangements were made with a local hotel to assure her basic shelter.

Technically the police obligation to Estelle should have ended with her arrest and presentation to court officials. Instead, officers made it their business to provide for her care upon return to the community. Other than an act of kindness, this type of follow up helped establish the credibility of the officers involved as individuals who were interested in protecting the interests of a person who was seemingly completely unable to cope with her situation.

• VICTIMS OF CRIME: A SPECIAL CONCERN

Since officers should also be especially sensitive to evidence of crisis in victims of criminal activity, we would suggest that part of the officer's responsibility at the crime scene is to be concerned with the mental health of the victim. Securing information necessary to determine if an offense has occurred, and, if so, to apprehend the offender, must become a secondary, though still vital concern.

Cohn (1973) reports in a study of 35 robbery victims that significant negative behavior changes were noted among some of the victims.

> In several instances, a general state of anxiety comes to permeate all activities, both at home and at work. Such people develop anxiety-reducing defenses, "limiting their ego activities," such as refraining from going out at night, avoidance of the place where the robbery took place, avoidance of young people who somehow remind the victim of the robbery; denial ("I've forgotten all about it") and obsessive thought processes ("I can't help thinking about it again and again"). (p. 21)

Cohn further reports certain "regressive trends" in the victims' behavior: a fear of going to the police; impairment of memory; negative physiological reactions such as "high temperature after the shock, sleeplessness, one of the victims had a stroke after the robbery, another is unable to eat, and others suffer from stomach[aches] and headaches." (p. 22)

Finally Cohn's study reveals that

> Many of the individuals interviewed accused the police and all official
> agencies of being ineffective and, what is worse, indifferent. One state-
> ment claimed that "everybody cares more for the robbers than they
> worry about us." Another expands this to society in general: "I tell my
> neighbors about what happened, but they immediately forget all about
> it." (p. 22)

Although the number of cases investigated by Cohn is small, the
general implications for police-community relations and the particular
responsibility that is placed on the investigating officers are clear. The
investigating officer should take a few extra minutes to assess the immediate impact of the encounter upon the victim.

Of course the officer may be facing a difficult decision—namely,
how much time should he devote to crisis intervention efforts if there
appear to be immediate prospects of apprehending the assailant or, in
fact, determining if a crime has occurred. Under these difficult circumstances, officers will make honest errors in judgment on either side of
the issue. The important factor, however, is that the interviewing officer
have a basic understanding of and confidence in the use of crisis intervention procedures when dealing with apparent victims of crime.

• MENTAL HEALTH
EMERGENCIES

A mental health emergency as opposed to a crisis situation is defined by Parad and Resnik (1975) as "a sudden, unforeseen, isolated
incident, which, if unresponded to, will result in life threatening or psy-
chologically damaging consequences." (p. 5)

Here the task of the officer is to stabilize the situation, preventing
the client from suffering further emotional damage or causing himself
or others physical injury. Once stability is achieved, the client usually
should be transferred to an appropriate hospital or mental health center.

Perhaps the most difficult task confronting the officer in this situation is the determination of whether such an emergency actually does
exist. Our society has become increasingly concerned with the right of
individuals who display bizarre behavior to be left alone.

Mental illness in itself, as the Cambridge, Mass. Police Department
has advised officers, does not warrant intervention by police unless the
individual has committed some criminal act or poses a clearly defined
threat to himself or others.

While the laws governing the right of the police to intervene in cases of suspected mental health emergencies vary from state to state, officers would be well advised to act only after directly observing specific acts on the part of the person said to be in need of help. Second-hand comments or observations from others do not provide a base for intervention.

Assuming that the officer has witnessed certain specific behaviors such as a clearly stated suicide intention, the next step must be to determine the seriousness or depth of the crisis facing the client.

The same basic steps apply when dealing with a non life-threatening crisis situation. Successful intervention requires, of course, establishing a relationship of trust with the client. The emergency situation is more difficult for the officer because the other individual may be in the depths of fear and confusion and may well mistrust the motives and actions of anyone approaching him.

The officer should proceed slowly and calmly, showing by his manner of speech and body movements that his attention is directed toward the person in distress; that he brings both competency and understanding to the situation. Patience is important. The client should be allowed to tell his or her own story at his own pace, carefully guided by the officer to disclose information that will aid the officer in making two basic judgments; how immediate is the danger to my client or others, and what action must be taken how soon.

If possible, the officer dealing with the potential suicide should attempt to determine if the client has any weapons or other dangerous objects. His initial concern should be for the safety of others and himself.

Assuming that the client is cooperative, attempts should be made to shift the discussion to a location of comparative quiet where the client may feel more at ease and the information gathering process may proceed under less pressure.

If it is clearly established that the client intends suicide or is so disoriented that he cannot care for himself, the officer should recommend to the client that he accept care in an inpatient facility. If the individual refuses such care and the officer is convinced that prompt action must be taken to protect the interests of the individual and others, force may be required. This is a most serious step and should not be taken by the officer without sure knowledge of the particular laws in his state which govern such acts.

Zusman (1975) comments,

This is a dangerous and complicated issue for several reasons. The threat or use of force by one person against another is a crime unless there are extenuating circumstances. . . . On the other hand, failure to use force or detain an obviously dangerous patient may leave you open to criticism or legal liability if the person then injures himself or another person. (p. 52)

If at all possible, the officer should attempt to consult with a mental health specialist before taking the step of detaining an individual against his will. Obviously, in some cases such communication is difficult or impossible, particularly in rural areas.

Therefore, it is imperative that any department, no matter how small, provide officers with training in identification and management of emergency situations involving the mentally ill. As with non life-threatening crises, the officer's role should be seen as akin to that of the first aid worker who provides help until full community resources can be obtained.

Case Three: Mental Health Emergency

Bertha W., age 40, separated from her husband, had been receiving state welfare assistance for herself and a daughter for some time. Under normal welfare procedures, state authorities had made direct payment of Bertha's rent to the Hopetown Housing Authority, the balance of the money being made available to her for general purposes. Suddenly state policies changed and monies were no longer paid directly to the housing authority but rather it was expected that Bertha, who now received the total check, had the ability to manage her own affairs and pay her rent. Because of an undefined emotional problem, Bertha was under the delusion that she was paying her rent, which was not the case. The housing authority had made numerous attempts to collect its rent. Bertha adamantly refused to make any payments.

Eviction proceedings were started. Bertha, in effect, barricaded herself in her apartment. Police, who had already experienced one direct physical confrontation with Bertha, were not anxious to repeat the exercise. Their dilemma was to secure the assistance of some competent authority who might reason with Bertha or be in a position to certify that she needed temporary mental health hospitalization. Staff of the local Health Department refused to intervene, saying that although they had prior information about Bertha's alleged mental inacapacity, they were unwilling to visit the scene and give an opinion. The director of Mental Health of a local hospital acknowledged that the police had a "difficult problem" but he was not willing to dispatch a staff member to assist. State welfare officials who had the power to act to protect the interests of the woman's daughter indicated that any action had to "go through channels."

The matter was finally resolved when a local sheriff in charge of evictions convinced Bertha that she might benefit by a vacation with her daughter in a distant state. Welfare funds were secured to provide for a one-way plane ticket and several cardboard suitcases. The city's problem with Bertha thus had been neatly solved. She was now the problem of the various police, welfare, and public health officials in another state.

Discussion • The problem facing the Hopetown police was their inability to secure expert advice that would allow them to enter Bertha's apartment under professional mental health supervision. The officers' main handicap in this particular situation was both the lack of cooperation from other agencies and the fact that Bertha had not committed any direct, observable acts or made any statements indicating violence against herself or other individuals. Nevertheless a mental health emergency clearly did exist.

This particular case clearly illustrates the suggestion made in Chapter 3 that it is absolutely vital that clear and consistent communication exist between the police and other helping agencies who have specialized knowledge—particularly in the instance of confirmed or suspected mental health emergencies.

Bertha's case really represents a travesty in interagency cooperation. Police spent a considerable amount of time debating various courses of action. Bertha's problem was never solved but merely passed on to another group of agencies who might well reciprocate the "favor" shown by Hopetown officials by eventually returning her to her original residence rather than providing the help she so desperately needed.

Case Four: Potential Suicide

Ida J., age 59, an immigrant from an eastern European country, had worked in the machine tool manufacturing industry as a laborer since age 21. Both of her parents were now deceased, and Ida lived with a brother, age 48, who made little contribution to their joint household. During a particularly short, sharp recession, Ida was laid off as an operator at the Webuildem Machine Tool Company after 15 years of continuous employment. She knew no other trade.

One morning, Officer Fitzpatrick, on foot patrol for several years in Ida's neighborhood, encountered her returning from a brief shopping errand. She obviously had been crying, her appearance was unkempt, and she was walking with a somewhat unsteady gait. Fitzpatrick who was known to Ida struck up the usual small talk conversation, quite deliberately, alerting himself to the fact that her usual appearance and outward behavior seemed markedly changed. "Ida, what's the matter?" You don't look like yourself." Ida replied with a lengthy tirade against Webuildem Company and recited her intense frustration at failing to find another job. Her unemployment compensation was within a few weeks of running out and her brother had contributed neither financial nor moral support. "Larry, there's nobody else in the world. I don't know what I'm going to do. I don't know anything else to do for a job. I'd be better off dead."

At this point, Fitzpatrick took stock of his previous knowledge of Ida, her actions, appearance, and attitude, and contrasted this with her present behavior. Gently but firmly, he took the crying woman to a nearby coffee shop and listened to her general complaints and suicidal threats in greater detail, at times interrupting her somewhat confused remarks with specific inquiries which focused her attention on the problems which seemed to bother her the most: the loss of a prized job, financial insecurity, and the lack of anyone to turn to.

Fitzpatrick rightly assumed that her suicidal threat, made in a context of confusion and despair, needed further professional evaluation. Quietly, but very specifically, he suggested that an appointment could be arranged with the Family Counseling Service located near Ida's neighborhood. Fitzpatrick suggested that Ida call a specific caseworker whom he had used quite successfully on other occasions.

Ida accepted the referral to the social worker who diagnosed her case as one not requiring immediate hospitalization but systematic, regular support through the agency. Although Ida's full sense of unhappiness could not be dealt with in a few short sessions, her intense sense of loneliness and insecurity, her ambivalence between life and death, was successfully approached, and she continued to maintain contact with Fitzpatrick's original referral source.

Fitzpatrick, within several days of his first referral, contacted the caseworker to find out if Ida had kept an appointment. She had. Several weeks later, Fitzpatrick made a second call to see if there were any appropriate role he or the police department might play in dealing with Ida's dilemma. While no assistance was requested, the caseworker gave a brief report, within the bounds of confidentiality, of Ida's progress. Total time elapsed in these phone conversations was probably no more than ten minutes, but Fitzpatrick had underscored his concern for Ida's welfare.

Discussion • This case, based on an actual situation, suggests several interesting points about police acting in mental health emergencies.

Although Fitzpatrick knew Ida and therefore was able to observe specific changes in her behavior, his quiet, thorough, and systematic approach could be used in identifying similar instances of mental health emergencies. Secondly, the result of Ida's case is quite real. It is not the Hollywood "all ends happily" result. Ida still had major problems to work through, all of which would take considerable time and patience on both her part and that of the caseworker. From the police point of view, the very real possibility of Ida's suicide had been averted. An efficient, thoughtful, and appropriate referral had been completed.

• CRISIS MANAGEMENT

While the terms crisis intervention and crisis management are often used interchangeably, we define crisis management as the police response to situations when officers act primarily as law enforcers rather than as helping agents.

Through crisis management, the officer or team of officers attempt to contain community conflict such as a fight between several groups of youths or adults or to prevent police contact with an individual lawbreaker from expanding into an uncontrollable situation.

The key to successful conflict management is law enforcement that keeps the community's peace, upholds the law, yet minimizes the use of force. While arrests may be necessary, they are undertaken as a last, not a first, resort.

Successful conflict management involves both preventive action on the part of the police and a controlled, systematic response to incidents that are unforeseen or unavoidable.

It is appropriate and important for a PCR unit or officer to attempt to identify community problems that may lead to confrontation between citizens, thus involving the police in an enforcement role.

During discussions with groups or individuals in conflict, the PCR unit should attempt to provide solutions to the dispute. Methods should be explored whereby dissenting groups can express their views in a manner that does not disturb the public peace. An example of this type of situation would be a labor dispute or a conflict between a group of tenants and a landlord.

It is important that the PCR unit carefully explain to any group planning a public demonstration the group's rights and obligations under the law. Police department policy should be made clear to all, not as a threat, but as a means of avoiding any confusion about police intentions.

Not all attempts of police to defuse potential conflicts will be successful. Groups may well distrust the intentions of the police or refuse to compromise; however, the task of the police should be to establish a clear and consistent record of willingness to work with community groups in resolving conflict.

Some conflicts are not predictable: a riot at a school sporting event; a neighborhood feud that has been smoldering and suddenly breaks into open conflict between several families. Here the task of the PCR unit is to help develop departmental tactics to meet the situation. Their goal is to minimize risk of injury to either participants or officers, to prevent the disturbance from spreading, and to use arrest in a precise, controlled manner.

A major goal of conflict management is to avoid the possibility of the responding officers becoming the focal point of the anger of both groups.

In order for police to maintain their stance as peace officers, it is vital that training in conflict management be provided for all officers. This should reflect the general tactical objectives of the department in meeting either anticipated or sudden conflicts among groups of individuals.

It is suggested that conflicts can best be managed by a police response that is proportional to the matter at hand. For instance, the dispatch of a large number of officers in riot gear to the scene of a small neighborhood disturbance would most likely produce the net result of police being viewed as heavy-handed and unsure of their ability to maintain the peace without a display of paramilitary force.

Summary: The Individual Officer and the Crisis Situation • The concepts of crisis intervention, mental health emergencies and conflict management need to be put into perspective.

Crisis intervention involves those situations of a non life-threatening nature. While the individual in crisis may recover the use of his coping (problem solving) ability unaided, positive intervention at the onset of the crisis will speed the recovery process and may avoid a repetition of the problem.

Police objectives should be to identify the cause of the distress, to assist the individual in meeting the impact of the crisis and to mobilize appropriate resources such as helping agency staff. The main objective for officers is to bring the case to a close as a police matter while securing the necessary help for those involved.

Emergency situations involve instances where the life of the client is threatened by his own actions, or where the person is so clearly incapable of caring for himself that some form of hospitalization is required.

In the latter instance, it is important that officers be carefully trained to recognize the difference between behavior that is simply unusual or unconventional and that which requires intervention. Secondly, police are under a significant obligation to remain with the individual until he is placed under the care of appropriate medical personnel.

Non life-threatening crises and emergencies are similar in that they impose a great degree of individual judgment on the part of the responding officer. These situations need to be viewed on a highly individual basis. It is vital that officers understand that their own attitudes and actions will play a major part in the outcome of a crisis or emergency intervention.

Crisis management involves those incidents to which officers respond in their role of law enforcers—peace keepers. These situations involve groups of individuals who have fallen into open conflict. The role of the line officer is to skillfully enforce the law and restore order without allowing his own feelings and attitudes to be drawn into the dispute.

• THE PCR UNIT'S ROLE

The PCR unit's responsibilities in developing a response to crisis and emergency situations are to identify and to develop line officers who will serve in a regular patrol capacity but with special skills in crisis situations.

Secondly, the PCR unit should make initial contact with civilian leadership and private helping agency personnel, explaining the department's crisis intervention program, its strengths and limitations, and securing from helping agencies in particular, specific commitments for acceptance of referrals.

The PCR unit should work with line officers in identifying those helping agencies that really will come to the aid of both officer and client. As stated earlier, line personnel should be encouraged to develop their own referral sources. When agencies who have promised help fail to deliver on a consistent basis the matter should be referred to the PCR unit, acting in a staff capacity. The unit should then deal directly with the agency in an attempt to secure delivery of services.

Because of their experience and training in the behavioral sciences, members of the PCR unit may serve in both line and staff roles when a department begins a crisis intervention program. We suggest that except where economics makes it impossible, the PCR unit should quickly "spin off" direct delivery of services to the line officers through specialized training. Larger departments may have both manpower and resources to allocate this assignment to a specialized crisis intervention unit or group of line officers whose sole duty is to handle a variety of disputes, particularly family crisis intervention.

• TRAINING FOR CRISIS INTERVENTION

There is a great similarity in the type of skills sought for both PCR and crisis intervention tasks. Officers should have a demonstrated interest in acting in a helping role; they should possess emotional maturity in the sense that the officer accepts responsibility for his actions and can live with outcomes which may be uncertain or disappointing from the intervener's point of view.

A non judgmental attitude is vital. It is essential that the officer be able to assess the situation facing his client without imposing his own subjective values. It is also important that the candidate possess patience and a willingness to explore every possible solution to the problem before breaking off contact, making a referral, or using the power of arrest.

The last point is important and should be carefully considered. Unlike other helpers, the officer has the power of lawful arrest. While one of the prime reasons for police to employ crisis intervention methods is to avoid arrest, the officer should not hesitate to use this authority when common sense indicates that a particular case may not be closed through the use of crisis intervention techniques.

Thus the successful police crisis intervention worker must accept his dual role: that of being primarily a helper but one who must also use his enforcement authority on occasion.

The Training Format • The use of persons not specifically trained in the mental health field (such as police officers) as crisis intervention agents is of such recent origin that no single training format has gained universal acceptance.

Shneidman (1973) suggests that three conditions are essential for effective development of lay persons as crisis interveners: careful selection, "rigorous training, and continuous ruthless supervision" (p. 11).

Motto, Brooks, Ross and Allen (1974) report that training programs for civilian crisis centers range from 18 to 48 hours with sessions being run up to 12 weeks for a series of three-hour, once a week classes.

While there are no hard and fast rules for training line officers in the tasks of intervention, the propositions suggested by Shneidman form a sound base for training officers. We would suggest a minimum of 30 hours of in-service training followed by weekly meetings of the crisis intervention team to review handling of actual cases in the field. Initial training should feature a heavy emphasis on non traditional resources such an extensive use of audio-visual material; analysis by trainees of actual taped or video taped crisis situations; role playing; and, if possible, observation of the operation of a community mental health center's crisis program. It would be valuable to have the training director or codirector from an agency that has had recognized success in training laymen in crisis intervention. It would be particularly helpful if this individual had worked closely and effectively with police officers.

Such a training program should focus on developing within each officer a range of responses to crisis situations and on strengthening his perceptions in recognizing crisis and emergency situations. Good intentions are not enough. In order for a department to undertake a systematic crisis intervention program, the rigorous standards suggested must be applied. Before each officer is assigned to crisis intervention duties, the trainer should attempt to evaluate the candidate on the basis of maturity, ability to make independent decisions, willingness to undergo high rates of stress, perception of client needs, and the ability to meet those needs directly or through an individualized referral.

The Team Approach • A successful program of crisis intervention rests on an understanding of goals and objectives between administrators, telephone operators-dispatchers, and the line officers who will carry out the actual intervention.

The administrator should be willing to accept the fact that interveners need a free hand in determining how much time is required to successfully terminate a particular crisis call. In turn, the administrator must establish a system of evaluation so that the effectiveness of each response can be measured.

Evaluation should start with weekly meetings of the intervention group. Here experiences can be shared to determine how general categories of crisis situations may be better managed.

Included in these sessions from time to time should be members of the department's communications unit. It is vital that these officers or similar civilian personnel be required to take part in the same training as the field crisis unit.

Most public calls for assistance come via telephone. The dispatcher, as one small department executive has remarked, "runs the show." A skillful dispatcher is needed to give line officers the essential details of the crisis situation. The dispatcher as well as the responding officer needs to be a perceptive listener—catching in the caller's manner and urgency the type of action that is necessary to meet the situation.

Perceptive, understanding listening and responding on the part of the operator may result in a problem being resolved by a direct referral by the operator rather than by dispatching officers. Calls that are often identified in official statistics as requests for information or "not police business" represent opportunities for the department to gain or lose community confidence. Clearly the caller has expected some form of response from the answering officer. The response should indicate, if at all possible, some alternative sources of referral or possibilities of help for the caller. The perceptive police administrator should encourage his communications unit to respond with courtesy, understanding, and as much genuine information as possible, even though the matter at hand does not require a police response.

It is important that the line officer understand the problems faced by the communications unit, namely the need to reply quickly and accurately when reporting progress or problems encountered in a crisis or mental health emergency situation. What is needed is an understanding by all officers that while they may play different roles in dealing with crises, a close knit team response will most likely bring the matter to a close as quickly as possible, thus releasing line officers to continue their regular duties.

Crisis Intervention: Not a Cure-all • The crisis intervention methods that we have described represent an improvement on traditional police responses to certain types of difficult service requests. If properly used, crisis intervention techniques tend to limit danger to officers, resolve the matter at hand more quickly, thus eliminating in part the number of repeat calls from "problem families" or chronic complainers. Perhaps more important, they provide the individual officer with the tools to turn an unpleasant task into a situation where positive lasting results can sometimes be seen by the line officer himself.

However, it should be clear that crisis intervention methods, whether practiced by mental health professionals, civilian volunteers, or police, have not been fully developed. They represent an advance in the art of interpersonal communications. They are not a scientifically designed series of steps that will always work when dealing with people who are upset, unreasonable, or even dangerous. Therefore it is important that when a crisis intervention program is undertaken by a department, expectations for success should be kept within bounds.

With this caution in mind, we would still suggest that crisis intervention techniques offer the police an opportunity to play a more effective role as mental health first aid agents. Crisis intervention training, programming, or the actual delivery of crisis services is therefore a vital, natural concern for any police-community relations program, for it underscores and strengthens the policeman's role as an effective helper in the community.

9

Community Justice: The Democratic Ideal

So far, a variety of topics relating to police-community relations have been discussed. We have defined PCR, looked at the full service model, examined the need for planning in PCR, and discussed PCR and its relation to other social service agencies. The present chapter will attempt a synthesis—exactly what is the relationship between the police and the community in a democratic society? We feel that it is imperative to understand PCR within the context of democracy in order to make a realistic and constructive statement.

What is a democracy? What is the police role in a democracy? To answer these questions, it is necessary to look at their respective origins. One cannot adequately understand the concept of democracy without first understanding the nature of social contract theory.[1] Berkley (1969) contends that social contract theory is "historically perhaps, the most significant element in democratic theory." (p. 4)

Social Contract Theory • The social contract theory was first elaborated by Locke and later by Rousseau and others. In effect, they rejected the then traditional doctrine that man owed absolute obedience to his government. Korn and McKorkle (1959) emphasize that obligations between man and government were analogous to a contract voluntarily entered into by free contractors.

---

[1] For a complete discussion on social contract theory, see Barker (1947).

133

It was the obligation of the State to protect the safety and promote the happiness of its constituent members. In return for these services, it was the obligation of the individual to surrender a small portion of his natural liberty in obedience to the valid laws of the State. The purpose of these laws—which express the obligations of the State—was to promote the greatest possible happiness for the greatest possible number. (p. 404)

Berkley (1969) comments:

Under this conception, the individuals agree as equals, to covenant together for their mutual benefit. They retain a right to withdraw from society, to abrogate the contract when they see fit. The contract theory thus implies equality, participation, consent, and consensus. (p. 4)

Thus, social contract theory is the basis, or at least the major element, in the theory of democracy. This is true because, as Berkley pointed out in the above paragraph, social contract theory implies equality, participation, and consent and consensus—the cornerstones of a democratic theory. Social contract theory has further implications for a society, particularly in the important area of social control.

Social Control Theory • Since men have come together freely for protection and security, it is necessary for the State to assume some form of control over the behavior of the members, so that the greatest happiness for the greatest number can occur. Social control may be defined as "the process by which subgroups and persons are influenced to conduct themselves in conformity to group expectations." (Davis, 1975, p. 17)

The State assumes the authority to guide and control behavior. Quinney (1970) points out that "authority relations are present in all social collectivities: some persons are always at the command of others. As order is established in a society, several systems of control develop to regulate the conduct of various groups of persons." (p. 36) As the contractors agree to form a union called State, it is necessary to give up a portion of their natural liberties so that the authority of the State may be established, and the good of the whole promulgated.

The State establishes its authority through the use of laws. The contractors freely accept and heed the system of laws created by the State. And, as Quinney further states "The legal system is the most explicit form of social control. The law consists of (1) specific rules of conduct, (2) planned use of sanction to support the rules, and (3) designated officials to interpret and enforce the rules." (p. 36)

Davis (1975) further defines law as the formal means of social control that involves the use of rules that are interpreted, and are enforceable, by the courts of a political community. Political community is defined by Max Weber (1954) as involving "Forcible maintenance of orderly dominion over a territory and its inhabitants." (p. 6)

Thus, we see the State exercising some form of control over the behavior of the members of the society. This authority to control is both implicit and explicit in the notion of social contract theory. Social control by the rule of law is the foundation of the modern criminal justice system. As a direct legal system, criminal justice (police, courts, corrections, and allied agencies) has been established by the authority of the rule of law for the expressed purpose of controlling human behavior. We could, therefore, say that the social control-criminal justice system has been established and maintained by the members of the society through their contractual participation in the social order.

Democracy—A Definition • Our discussion thus far has touched on several elements of a democracy. We have indicated that social contract theory, social control theory, and the rule of law are all parts of a definition of democracy. Berkley (1969) has pointed out that there are other common elements of a democracy. They may be summarized as follows:

1 · Consensus · the first requirement of a democracy. The consent of the governed is the precondition for a particular democratic government. And certainly this is the fundamental element so necessary in social contract theory. Berkley indicates that "government activity in a democracy is conceived as resulting from the demands of, or at least with the consent of, those whom the activity is designed to serve." (p. 3)

2 · Freedom · certainly a basic requirement to a functioning democracy. Men must be free in order to enter into a true contractual relationship. Freedom here implies equality among participating members of the society. And freedom would also imply that each member does have an actual amount of participation and consent in the society. As Cicero points out, freedom is participation in power.[2]

In sum, Lincoln's proposition that democracy is government of the people, by the people, and for the people seems an accurate description of the essence of the democratic ideal.

---

[2] Reported in George Berkley, *The Democratic Policeman* (Boston: Beacon Press, 1969), p. 3.

Interest Groups and Politics • Certainly the above definition would seem adequate, at least philosophically, for the American brand of democracy. Yet, there are two other vital issues that must be involved in our discussion: the notions of interest groups and of politics.

Interest groups certainly characterize the American form of democracy. Interests or interest groups are segments of the society that have particular goals or needs which they attempt to fill through the democratic process. Quinney (1970) notes: "Each segment of society has its own values, its own norms, and its own ideological orientations. When these are considered to be important for the existence and welfare of the respective segments, they may be defined as interests." (p. 38) Thus, interests are grounded in the various segments, parts or groups which make up the society and represent their particular individualistic concerns. Interests are characteristic of American democracy. One has only to consider the special lobby groups in Washington, D.C. Clearly, the consumer advocate groups, the oil interests, the AMA, the ABA, and so forth are examples of interest groups on a national scale. On a local scale, we may see the Chamber of Commerce, the neighborhood association, or the municipal employees group as examples of local interests. The individuals comprising these groups attempt to achieve their interests via the democratic process.

Yet, Quinney is quick to point out, this process is not always democratic.

> The interest structure is characterized by the unequal distribution of power and conflict among the segments of the society. It is differentiated by diverse interests and by the ability of the segments to translate their interests into public policy. Furthermore, the segments are in continual conflict over their interests. Interests thus are structured according to differences in power and are in conflict. (p. 39)

Politics is also characteristic of American democracy. It may be defined as the ability of the segmented group to achieve and maintain their interests. It is the process of transforming or translating the private into the public policy. And, as Quinney has pointed out, the ability of the segment to accomplish this depends on the group power and its adroitness in influencing the democratic process. Thus, the groups which are essentially the "haves" who maintain power over the "have-nots" are the ones who are able to effect a public policy which is reflective of their own private interests.

So, what does democracy mean? As we have already indicated, democracy implies consent of the governed to be governed; it implies a notion of freedom and equality in which one makes choices—free choices—in deciding upon the contractual arrangements. We have said that democracy, in its pure form, is government of the people, by the people, and for the people. We have also indicated that there are at least two other elements in democracy, American style—interests and politics. We have said that a "power elite" (Mills, 1956) controls the democratic process by influencing public policy which is reflective of particular private interests.

• POLICE IN A DEMOCRATIC SOCIETY

The police in a democratic society represent a variety of problems to the society, at least philosophically. The very nature of what the police do and how they are organized creates problems for democracy. Thus, Skolnick (1966) writes:

> The police in a democratic society are required to maintain order and to do so under the rule of the law. As functionaries charged with maintaining order, they are part of the bureaucracy. The ideology of the democratic bureaucracy emphasizes initiative rather than disciplined adherence to rules and regulation. By contrast, the rule of law emphasizes the rights of individual citizens and constraints upon the initiative of legal officials. This tension between the operational consequences of ideas of order, efficiency, and initiative, on the one hand, and legality, on the other, constitutes the principal problem of the police as a democratic legal organization. (p. 6)

The police are thus cast into the difficult position of having to maintain law and order through the rule of law. On the one hand, law provides a set of rules for the maintenance of order—"the elements of crime, the principles under which the accused is to be held accountable for alleged crime, the principles justifying the enactment of specific prohibition, and the crimes themselves" (Skolnick, p. 7). On the other hand, law regulates the conduct of the police and other legal agents charged with the processing of accused citizens; "laws of search, law of arrest, the elements and degree of proof, the right to counsel, the nature of a lawful accusation of crime, and the fairness of trial" (Skolnick, p. 8).[3]

This apparent dichotomy presents a dilemma to the police. They are charged with efficiency in maintenance of order, yet they are re-

---

[3] From *Justice Without Trial* by J. Skolnick. New York: Wiley, 1966. Copyright 1966. Reprinted by permission of John Wiley & Sons, Inc.

stricted and limited by the very order they are to maintain. Democracy
for the police is a harsh task master. Police are mandated to enforce
laws, yet are not given the total authority necessary for the efficient
accomplishment of the order.

Berkley (1969) points to still further problems in connection with
police functioning and the democratic ideal. "The police more than any
other institution exhibit an antagonism, both in concept and practice,
to some of the basic precepts of a democratic society. In many respects,
the phrase 'democratic police force' is a contradiction in terms." (p. 2)

Consensus • The policeman's job, as Berkley so aptly points out, begins
when "consensus fails to work: the less the consensus, the more police
power." (p. 2) Furthermore, "government authority is often conceptual-
ized in democracy as a result from a bestowal from the clientele to the
agency, the clientele of the police make no such bestowal. In fact, they
stubbornly resist." (p. 3)

Freedom • The policeman does not meet the citizen on equal footing,
claims Berkley. Social control theory indicates that individuals come
together to form a State for a variety of purposes. Implicit in this agreement is the ability to withdraw from the contract. The same follows for
our social encounters with each other. Most social encounters are vol-
untary, each party coming together, always maintaining the right to
disengage himself from the encounter at any time. When the policeman
encounters a citizen, the right, the freedom to withdraw, vanishes. Thus,
the exercise of police power is at variance with the elements of freedom
and equality.

In sum, we can see that the role of the police in a democratic
society is a difficult one at best. The police seem to represent the exact
antithesis of democracy. They are required to maintain an orderly,
safe society. They receive their authority to do so by the rule of law.
Yet, as we have pointed out, maintenance of order and the rule of
law may be at odds with each other. Pure, perfect order maintenance
may be obtained realistically through a variety of methods, most of
which would be in direct violation of the rule of law. Law is designed
both to protect and to punish. As Chwast (1973) points out, the debate
over the relationship between ends and means is a recurring one. The
dilemma that the police find themselves in, of course, is whether or not
the end justifies the means.

Perhaps the problem is not as serious as it initially sounds. Examining the social control process, we see that individuals freely come
together to form the State. We also see that these individuals must give

up a certain amount of their natural rights for the good of the whole. Implicit in this is the ability of the State to guide and influence the behavior of the members for the greatest happiness. This guiding function is social control. The chief form of social control in society is vested in the legal code. Part of the legal code is the notion of sanction. This is where the police come in. The Criminal Justice System in general, and the police in particular, are charged with direct social control over the members of the State, so that the greatest good may be established. Thus, it is the democratic responsibility of the police to maintain the good (order). Those individuals who break the law(s), essentially void their contract and act in an undemocratic manner in the sense that they undermine the good of the society. Thus, the police serve the vital democratic function of maintaining the society by social control over the members.

And yet, this still does not solve our problem. In the above sense, does the end justify the means? The answer to this must be an emphatic *NO!* Further insight into the problem is necessary. Because of the manner in which the police carry out their roles, it would seem that their behavior directly violates the elements of democracy. This places the policeman in a grossly different role from anyone else in society. As Berkley (1969) points out:

> The policeman does not meet the citizen on equal footing. Instead, he is equipped with additional power stemming not only from the authority, both formal and informal, of his office but also from the tools of his trade. All policemen carry weapons and have the right to use them. (p. 3)

Skolnick (1966), too, contends that the authority the police officer has in enforcing laws and maintaining order tends to isolate the officer from the larger society (p. 44). This isolation and alienation may lead to the "we-they" dichotomy where the police and the rest of the society are pitted against each other. This would certainly seem to explain the common situation of hostility between the police and the public so often discussed in the literature (e.g. Fink & Sealy, 1974). Doig (1968), commenting on this, states:

> This concern with the political impact of the police is directed toward at least two different aspects of the police role. First, the policing function itself is seen as involving substantial discretion; decisions are made and modified down through the lowest ranks on how force and the threat of force will be used, on how individual liberty and privacy will be safeguarded or abrogated. The police have a significant, direct role . . . in determining the relationship of the citizen to his government. (p. 394)

Thus, the dilemma of efficient order maintenance and the rule of law exists not so much in the sense that law, or certain laws, must be enforced, but rather, *the manner in which they are enforced.* It would seem that in fact there is no dichotomy between the rule of law and order maintenance. Is there any reason why the police cannot efficiently maintain order within the rule of law? Perhaps it is the problem of discretion, as Doig has indicated, that creates the problem for both the police and the public.

• POLITICS AND THE ROLE OF THE POLICE

Another way to examine the problem is within the context of police role functioning and role attitudes. Goldstein (1968) points out:

> The traditional police approach has been to emphasize crime control in recruitment and training and in rewarding policemen; service activities which actually consume the majority of police time, have been viewed as burdensome and largely inappropriate for police officers. (p. 395)

Since police officers are recruited, trained, and rewarded for crime control activities, there is evidence that many of them approach the numerous service activities with the attitude that this is not "real" police work. Therefore, the manner in which the police officer approaches the service duties creates problems—problems of democracy—for the police officer. And a large proportion of order maintenance activity is comprised of these service duties. J. Q. Wilson (1968) comments that "most order-maintenance situations do not result in an arrest—the parties involved wish the officer to 'do something' that will 'settle things,' but they often do not wish to see the settlement entail an arrest." (p. 407) It is precisely this type of situation that seems to be creating the conflict. Police officers, to repeat, have been recruited, trained, and rewarded according to crime control activities and arrest. Yet Wilson indicates that in most police activities an arrest is often not desired by the complaining party.

Skolnick (1966) helps shed some light on this problem. He indicates:

> Order under law suggests procedures different from achievement of "social control" through threat of coercion and summary judgment (arrest). Order under law is concerned not merely with the achievements of regularized social activity but with the means used to come by peace-

able behavior, certainly with procedure but also with positive law. (p. 9) [4]

Thus, the conflict may be resolved by viewing order and legality as complementing each other rather than conflicting with each other. Positive (democratic) social order is possible and practical for the police to maintain, provided that they approach policing from this point of view.

In order to facilitate positive social order, democratization of the police force is essential. This may be achieved in a variety of ways, both internally and externally.

In the internal sense, new role definitions must be developed for the police officer. Order maintenance will not necessarily be achieved through the use of force and coercion. The police role must also be understood to consist of a positive helping approach as well as a coercive function. This helping approach, outlined in Chapter 2, emphasizes that order under law is a positive democratic phenomenon.

Unfortunately, both the police themselves and the public often perceive the police role as negative—always enforcing, coercing, etc. What must be emphasized is the many positive things that policemen do. Emphasis here needs to be made both to the police officer in his training and to the public. Both the police and the public need to conceive of the police role as a positive element in democracy.

An external change that the police could make is in the area of politics. Police participation in politics can be viewed as a positive element, serving to bring the police back closer to society. Niederhoffer and Blumberg (1973) suggest that the concepts of police and politics are not necessarily alien.

> The derivation of the two words shows that there is close affinity. Police is derived from the Greek word Politeia, meaning citizenship and connoting the control and regulation of a political unity such as a nation or a state. Similarly, politics comes from the Greek word Politikos, meaning citizen: its definition is the art or science dealing with the regulation and control of men living in society. (p. 9)

Thus, police participation in politics may not be the negative process that most of us envision. Berkley (1969) comments on this:

---

[4] From *Justice Without Trial* by J. Skolnick. New York: Wiley, 1966. Copyright 1966. Reprinted by permission of John Wiley & Sons, Inc.

Participation in politics and political organizations, however, does offer many possibilities for promoting police democratization. For one thing, it erases a distinction between the policeman and his fellow citizens. Participation in democratic politics tends to strengthen democratic values in the participant and reinforce democratic attitudes. (p. 173)

Perhaps political participation on the part of both the individual police officer and the police organization may achieve a positive contribution toward democracy. Manning (1971) has suggested that the police are very closely tied to the political system in three ways:

1 · The police are an integral part of the political system because the vast majority of American police are locally controlled. By far, the greatest number of police officers are directed and otherwise controlled by local politicians.

2 · The police are an integral part of the political system because law is a political entity, and the administration of criminal law unavoidably encompasses political values and political ends. Thus, the police directly serve the political ends of the interest group in power. Perhaps the most outstanding example of this may be found during prohibition. The police were required to enforce certain laws pertaining to the manufacture, sale, and consumption of alcoholic beverages. Prohibition legislation was a direct result of a certain powerful interest group of the times.

3 · The police are an integral part of the political system because the police must administer the law.

Manning further states:

Because law enforcement is for the most part locally controlled, sensitivity to local political trends remains an important element in police practice. Since the police are legally prohibited from being publicly political, they often appeal to different community groups, and participate sub rosa in others, in order to influence the determination of public policy. (p. 167)

Thus, the police, whether by design or not, are tied closely to the ruling political structure. Also, in most communities the police constitute a powerful interest group whose activities are partially hidden from public view. Since the police are so obviously tied to the political structure, why not allow them to participate fully and openly in the political process?

Democratic politics, Berkley writes, "are generally characterized by negotiation and bargaining, by accommodation and conciliation, and offer little opportunity for the wielding of naked, unfettered power." (p. 173) Allowing the police to participate openly in the political process would be a positive contribution to strengthening democracy.

Political participation remains but one of the several methods of democratization of the police. Yet, the democratic process is so closely tied to the political system as to be indistinguishable. By far, overt police participation in the political structure is the most important of all forms or strategies of democratization of the police. The police contribution, albeit, the police interest, remains to be seen and directly felt. At least on the surface, it would appear that police social and political leadership will have much to contribute to the overall functioning of the society. The police have much to offer; who else, as a group are more actively aware of the pressing social problems and decay within our urban environments? The police know and, we might add, have known for years. It is time for the public to recognize this knowledgeable and experienced group, in order that they too may fully participate in the social order.

• THE DEMOCRATIC POLICEMAN IN THE COMMUNITY

One might ask what democracy has to do with police-community relations? We would contend that democracy, implying equal participation in government, requires that police officers as public citizens have the cooperation of all other citizens. In order to achieve social order in a democracy, it is necessary for both the police and the community to participate. Clifford and Morris (1973) echo this theme and indicate the necessity for strong cooperation between the police and the community. Prevention of crime and delinquency, and we might add, the preservation of the social order, is dependent upon both the police *and* other community members.

> The prevention and control of crime and delinquency involve a multiplicity of official and community agencies. The usual control organizations are the police, the courts and the correctional agencies. But if we look at the wider aspects of social defense, we are inexorably led to consider almost the entire spectrum of social organization. The family and its support by government and the local community, the school, the church, the organization of industry and transport, the structure of social services—all of these and much else are relevant to the prevention and treatment of crime and delinquency. . . . One perspective on the relationship between police and governmental roles in the treatment of crime and delinquency is to see criminal law as a control of and limitation on individual and community self-help against disruptive, discordant and unacceptable be-

havior. But if it is to be at all effective, the centralization of such authority (police) requires acceptance by the local community and hence some
degree of public support. (pp. 164, 166)

Riley (1973) offers further comment on the necessity of cooperation
between the public and the police: "first, no laws can be enforced or
order kept successfully unless the police and the community cooperate
with each other; and secondly, today in our urban ghettos there is very
little of that necessary mutual cooperation and support" (p. 195). This
presents a difficult situation. On the one hand, if order is to be maintained
in the society, the public and the police must cooperate with each other.
Yet, Riley points to the fact that such relationships are largely non-existent
in the urban ghetto. The riots of the 1960s serve as national testimony to
this disturbing fact. What such correspondents as Clifford and Morris
(1973) and Riley (1973) are telling us is that we absolutely must rely
on community cooperation and support if the police are to achieve their
assigned task. The assigned task is to maintain order under law. Certainly the police could maintain order without community support, as any
totalitarian society has shown. It is doubtful and indeed impossible for
the police to maintain order *under law* without community support.

Albert Reiss (1971) in *The Police and the Public* offers an interesting variation on the present discussion. In his account of citizen initiated
encounters which comprised 93.1 percent of all police activity in his study,
Reiss indicates that the citizens exercise a considerable amount, if not the
major amount, of discretion over police activity.

The data in Table 9.1 indicates the percent of citizen initiated encounters by type of incident and specific setting. Analysis indicates that,
at a minimum for felony calls, the police must be requested to come to
an enclosed private place within a dwelling 43 percent of the time. What
this indicates, of course, is that the police must rely on the public to bring
to their attention almost half (and probably more if one considers the 27
percent of calls concerning a felony in an open private place) of all known
felony cases. One must remember that the police are charged with maintaining order within the community. Given the fact that citizens exercise
a considerable amount of discretion over reporting criminal activity and in
general requesting services from the police, the police must maintain good
relationships with other community members in order to fulfill their democratic function. Certainly we can see that the police must rely on community members for their cooperation at least in informing the police of
criminal activity and in requesting other types of services. The police will
be unable to maintain order, effective order, under law without the cooperation of the citizenry.

Table 9.1   Percentage of Citizen Initiated Encounters According to the General Type of Incident, by Specific Setting of Encounter

Specific Setting of Encounter	General Type of Incident									
	Felony	Misde-meanor	Traffic Viola-tion	Juve-nile Trouble	Suspi-cious Person or Situ-ation	Non-Crimi-nal Dispute	Serv-ice	Un-founded	Other	All Inci-dents
Enclosed private place: within dwelling	43	35	6	16	38	55	37	27	47	36
Open private place: porch, yard, etc.	27	33	37	53	37	31	35	34	23	34
Semipublic place: within business	8	10	1	6	7	7	3	14	2	7
Semipublic place: other	5	4	4	3	1	*	10	3	2	5
Open public place	17	18	52	22	16	7	14	21	19	18
Total percentage	100	100	100	100	99	100	99	99	100	100
Total number	(554)	(637)	(154)	(346)	(73)	(467)	(553)	(157)	(47)	(2,988)

* 0.5 percent or less.

Reprinted from: Albert J. Reiss, Jr. *The Police and the Public.* New Haven: Yale University Press, 1971, p. 16.

145

• COMMUNITY
JUSTICE

What all of this points to, certainly, is a notion that policing in a democratic society can be accomplished only with the cooperation and support of all citizens. As we have pointed out, it is possible, at least theoretically, for the police to maintain order in a society without the cooperation of the public. Numerous examples may be cited—Hitler's Germany and Stalin's U.S.S.R. to name but a few. But to achieve order under law, it is necessary to have total community support for the maintenance of the society.

The notion of community justice seems to well summarize policing in a democratic society. Democracy implies, if not requires, mutual participation in government by the society. If government in a democracy is of the people, by the people and for the people, *law*, and therefore its enforcement, is the principle means of regulating conduct in the democracy. Laws reflect the attitudes of the people or at least specific groups of people. Law is designed to achieve order *for* the people.

The people, and one must be aware that the police *are* people, are ultimately responsible for policing in their community. It is responsibility implict in the contractual aspects of democracy. The ideal of community justice envisions the entire community working to maintain order under law.

We have thus attempted to show the relationship between democracy and police-community relations. We have indicated that in a democratic society the people are responsible for maintaining order under law. The concept of community justice implies the police, the criminal justice system and the community (people) working in harmony to produce order under law so that the ideal of democracy—the greatest happiness for the greatest number—may be achieved.

(10)

Toward Real
Police–Community
Relations

This book has attempted to review the existing state of police-community relations programs and make some specific proposals for revamping the concept of police-community relations. The PCR officer, unit, and/or team have been designated as vital instruments in the overall police function. Yet the term "police-community relations" is viewed in many segments of most communities with attitudes which range from skepticism and hostility to outright apathy.

The bright hopes and enthusiasm of many police administrators that community relations programs might provide a viable link with "them," the other citizens of the community, are largely dead. As Brown (1973) suggests, traditional police-community relation efforts have largely failed in black communities. A former policeman and past director of a San Jose, California PCR unit, Brown contends that "Black people will not identify with a police department which they see as over-policing and under-protecting the Black community." (p. 121)

Police-community relations also has a hollow ring to residents of upper middle-class white neighborhoods mainly populated by those over 50 years of age, who perceive that their neighborhood is being inundated by incidents of breaking and entering, purse snatching, and mugging. These individuals are not convinced by contrived neighborhood meetings presided over by unfamiliar youthful police-community relations officers waving computer printout sheets which state that crime in their neighborhood has increased insignificantly over the past few months so there is really nothing to worry about.

There is something to worry about. Whether through increased efficiency in reporting or an actual rise in incidents, crime, what we call hard crime—that is, attacks against persons and their personal property—appears to be rising out of control in the view of many citizens.

Some Major Problems • Not only do crimes seem to be increasing, but as indicated earlier, the credibility of police efforts seems to be in doubt, particularly in many of our major metropolitan areas. In 1974 the U.S. Department of Justice released data on a survey of victimization in the nation's five largest cities (Chicago, Detroit, Los Angeles, New York and Philadelphia). A significant number of citizens interviewed indicated that they had not reported instances of victimization to police for the following three major reasons: "nothing could be done [because there was] lack of proof"; "not important enough"; "police would not want to be bothered" (p. 5).

Thus, despite more than a decade of various types of police-community relations programs (at least in our major cities) there appears to be a sense of helplessness, a feeling that crime is a part of everyday life or that the citizen's problems are not important enough to be called to police attention and that officers would not welcome such a report.

However, there is every evidence that while citizens are concerned about perceived increases in crime they still demand by their service requests that police time be spent carrying out various helping functions. As larger departments in particular have developed 911 emergency telephone systems, it seems that the volume of these service calls has increased. Thus the task of genuine police-community relations efforts is to move beyond cosmetic pacification programs toward efforts which make police work in dealing with both law enforcement and service requests more effective for individual citizens, more rewarding for individual officers, and more successful in achieving departmental goals and community demands.

No matter how client-oriented a police department is in its relationship with citizens, we suggest that there will always be a gap between the police and the policed. When all the niceties are stripped away, and allowing for the large amount of police time spent on human service activities, the policeman is still the individual in the community who frequently has to say "no" to a citizen as he goes about some aspect of his business. In short, there is no way of glossing over the fact that the police are the first line of authority for the state.

This natural level of tension, it seems, has been heightened in recent years by the movement of police to seek the social recognition of professionals—the same drive that has occurred among public employees at many levels.

Michael Banton (1974) relates an anecdote that suggests a partial resolution of the tension between citizens and policemen: A Scottish police officer remarked in a discussion at the Scottish Police College, "The essence of a good cop is the man who can book a man in the morning and be able to hold a friendly conversation with him in the evening" (p. 309).

• A WORKABLE PCR MODEL

A workable model for a police-community relations program involves both in-house and general public aspects. The in-house aspect is a systematic effort to help officers realize that they *are*, as Banton (1974) suggests, simply "men with a job to do." (p. 309) The officer must realize he is a professional public servant, not mandated to undertake a crusade against crime but to fulfill a complex variety of duties—tasks that are necessary and vital if our democratic society is to function in some sort of civilized fashion. It is equally important that the citizen have confidence that the officer who confronts him in either a helping or enforcement capacity is not doing so for purely personal reasons, that he is simply "a man with a job to do," and that he is undertaking that task as a legitimate representative of the total community.

One of the most vital factors in the police officer's being recognized as a professional is that the line officer must *internalize* the values associated with professionalism—namely willingness to expose himself to new ideas and methods, and to approach his job with an attitude of community service. As a professional the officer must develop a strong sense of ethical values but also be able to deal with a diversity of situations and people in an unbiased manner.

One of the key tasks for police-community relations is to encourage officers to be fully participating citizens within the community that they police. It is vital that the line police officer feel not only free but encouraged to articulate his views when matters of general community controversy arise. This means full and active participation in the political process, participation that can be carried out without fear of reprisal from administrators or politicians. When police act as fully participating citizens they are less likely to be seen as an army of occupation, attempting only to police.

Having advocated a role of full citizenship for the police officer, it naturally follows that citizenship is a two-way street. Namely, police officers and departments as a whole must be more willing to accept soundly based public criticism and scrutiny more graciously than they have in the past. If the individual policeman wants the status of a professional and the full rights of other citizens, he must be willing to deal openly with the insistence and even demands of other citizens that they have a direct say in the operation of the most visible of all governmental services—the police.

A Sharing of Power • The ultimate question in police-community relations therefore concerns power. Police, for their part, must be willing to abandon the stance that they know what is best for the community in terms of law enforcement priorities. They must recognize that while citizen participation is admittedly tiresome and at times unwelcome from their point of view, it is a necessary process if they are to obtain their stated goals of enforcing the law and keeping the peace.

All citizens, including youth and minority group members, must develop some degree of trust in their police officers. A number of strategies and procedures have been suggested which will make a sharing of trust between police and citizens more probable. However, these strategies are not in themselves a panacea for achieving lasting, demonstrable change between the police and the policed. Perhaps there needs to be a growing awareness that in our imperfect society the expectations of both police officers and citizens will never be fully realized. Police will never be able to provide the degree of freedom from crime and violence that the citizen expects. Nor will the police officer attain the automatic trust and respect of all members of the community. Police-community relations, at its best, provides a vehicle for the lessening of tensions between the police officer and the citizen. That the tension exists is, in fact, a normal healthy product of a free, diverse, and open society.

Some Basic Changes • With this awareness, we have suggested the following changes in emphasis in police-community relations efforts:

1 · Expanding police efforts in consumer evaluation of police, law enforcement, and social services. Emphasis should be placed on anticipating real community problems as well as identifying citizens fears and perceptions of what is troubling the community.

2 · Building strong, working relationships with community social service agencies so that service requests may be systematically and appropriately referred or dealt with, thus maximizing police time on the line in dealing with law enforcement problems.

3 · Recognizing and utilizing psychology and crisis intervention skills in handling of nonenforcement situations.

4 · Paying increasing attention to the prolonged effects of stress, particularly on the line officer. One of the prime tasks of the PCR unit should be to act as in-house crisis interveners to offer appropriate assistance and encouragement to the line officer who often performs physically and mentally taxing tasks.

5 · Finally, there must be an awareness on the part of all police, particularly the line officers, of the effects of police behaviors on members of the community. The in-house task of fostering this attitude, it has been suggested, is just as vital as efforts to form good relationships with the civilian community.

Despite the *perceptions* of social scientists in the late 1960s, there is strong evidence, as indicated earlier, that a considerable reservoir of *general* support for police exists in inner city areas as well as in suburban and rural communities. The problem of the police, particularly in the inner city, appears to be translating this general level of support into willingness of citizens to report crimes more frequently, and to see the task of establishing and supporting community justice as the business of every citizen. The sense of community involvement will be fostered when individual police departments can translate police-community relations from something more than a rather pleasant concept into an ongoing function of every member of the department.

Glossary

COMMUNICATION • The process in which individuals share with one another their real feelings and concerns regarding a specific issue. Good communication features clarity and precision of thought by all parties.

COMMUNITY PROFILE PROJECT • A program of the San Diego Police Department initially funded by the Police Foundation that attempts to upgrade the status and performance of the beat officer by requiring that he develop an intimate working knowledge of his patrol area.

CONSUMER FEEDBACK • A process in which an organization, in this case the police, receives information concerning public attitudes and reactions to their services. Feedback may be obtained through a variety of testing devices.

COPING • The process in which all individuals deal with certain problem situations. The individual who is unable to respond effectively to a problem is said to be experiencing a failure of his coping ability and may be in a state of crisis.

CRISIS INTERVENTION • Actions taken by police, laymen, or mental health professionals to assist an individual in coming to terms with a particular personally unmanageable problem. Intervention is seen as a form of mental health first aid.

CRISIS MANAGEMENT • A condition that involves police intervention in conflict situations where their initial role is to act as law enforcers and maintainers of public order.

CYNICISM • An attitude held by an individual in which human actions and behavior are regarded with suspicion, distrust, and a lack of hope. Cynicism among police is said to result from the disproportionate amount of time they spend dealing with individuals who are either lawbreakers or social manipulators.

EVALUATION • The process by which a particular program or group such as a PCR unit is studied to determine its effectiveness in fulfilling stated goals.

FULL SERVICE MODEL • A view of police work which suggests that order maintenance and helping functions of a department are just as important as traditional enforcement tasks in meeting public expectations of service.

HELPING PROFESSIONAL • A person engaged in assisting others through a variety of social agencies such as the police department, medical personnel, social workers, and mental health agents. The professional is distinguished from other workers by his dedication to a specific code of ethics, community service, and willingness to undergo specific training.

HUMAN BEHAVIOR TRAINING • Instruction offered either through academic institutions or police academies whereby the officer is informed about certain basic elements regarding human actions and reactions in certain specific situations.

HUMAN RELATIONS TRAINING • Training that differs from that of the behavioral sciences because it generally attempts to create an empathetic attitude in an individual toward another social group in the community.

IN-HOUSE TASKS • The process by which an organization transmits information or deals with problems of organization members so that the total group functions in a more efficient manner.

JOHN WAYNE SYNDROME • The concept advanced by psychologist Martin Reiser stating that younger police officers tend to act aggressively in order to fulfill what they assume is the tough guy image of the effective police officer.

LATERAL ENTRY • The process by which a police officer can directly enter a certain position within a department without having first served an apprenticeship role.

MENTAL HEALTH EMERGENCY • A situation in which the life or mental health of an individual will be directly threatened unless crisis intervention action is promptly and efficiently taken.

ORDER MAINTENANCE • Police actions which are designed to contain and defuse a disruption of community peace with a minimal number of arrests.

PARTICIPATION TRAINING MODEL • A technique which assumes that learning is aided by trainees taking part in role playing or group experiences rather than listening to formal lecture-style training presentations.

POLICE-COMMUNITY RELATIONS • A service concept which assumes the need to maintain continuous open communication with the public and other service agencies.

POLICE CULTURE • A patterned set of beliefs and actions which are said to separate police work from other occupations.

POLICE ISOLATION • The result of the perceptions of many officers that they are actively disliked by other members of the community. Allegedly this leads to police socializing only with each other and placing organizational interests above community interests.

POLITICS • The ability of a particular group to achieve and maintain their interests in the community.

PUBLIC RELATIONS • The communication device by which an organization such as the police attempts to convince others that the work they are doing is important, needs support, and is being carried out in a highly efficient fashion.

REAL POLICE WORK • Duties that are often viewed by many officers as excluding helping functions. Stress is placed on the law enforcement role of both officer and department.

ROLE CONFLICT • A situation that arises when one's expectations concerning a job are not met. Contrary demands are seen as dominating the job task causing a perceived gap between job theory and reality.

ROLE PLAYING • A learning mechanism by which an individual acts out his feelings toward another person or group or attempts to put himself in the place of a person with differing views and attitudes. Often used as a training mechanism to determine and change the views or reactions of police recruits and veteran officers.

RULE OF LAW • The concept in which the police officer is viewed as an agent of the total community who must act in a manner which respects the legal and moral rights of all members of the community. This means that the law enforcer enjoys no special privileges in carrying out his duties.

SIGNIFICANT OTHERS • Those individuals, often friends or relatives, who are frequently contacted by a police officer to help his client deal with a crisis situation. Particular care should be taken to make sure that the significant others will play a helpful role in resolving the problem.

Bibliography

Adams, T. F. *Law enforcement: An introduction to the police role in the criminal justice system.* Englewood Cliffs, N.J.: Prentice-Hall, Inc., 1968.

Ahern, J. F. Reported in C. D. Engle, Police training in non-crime related functions. *The Police Chief,* June 1974, *41*, 61-66.

Avila, D. L. On killing humanism and uniting humaneness and behaviorism. *American Psychologist,* 1972, *27*, 579.

Badalamente, R. V., Clay, G. E., Halterlein, P. J., Jackson, T. T. Moore, S. A., & Rio, P. Training police for their social role. *Journal of Police Science and Administration,* 1973, *1*, 440-453.

Banton, M. Policing a divided society. *The Police Journal,* 1974, *46*, 309-321.

Bard, M. Family intervention police teams as a community mental health resource. *Journal of Criminal Law, Criminology, and Police Science,* 1969, *60*, 247-250.

Bard, M. *Training police as specialists in family crisis intervention.* Washington, D.C.: U.S. Government Printing Office, 1970.

Bard, M., & Berkowitz, B. A community psychology consultation in public family crisis intervention: preliminary impressions. *International Journal of Social Psychiatry,* 1969, *15*, 213.

Barker, E. (Ed.). *Social contract: essays by Locke, Hume, and Rousseau.* London: Oxford University Press, 1947.

Bazelon, D. L.   Psychologists in corrections—are they doing good for the offender or well for themselves? In S. L. Brodsky. *Psychologists in the criminal justice system.* American Association of Correctional Psychologists, 1972.

Bergin, A. E.   The evaluation of therapeutic outcomes. In A. E. Bergin & S. L. Garfield (Eds.). *Handbook of psychotherapy and behavior change.* New York: Wiley, 1971.

Berkley, G.   *The democratic policeman.* Boston: Beacon Press, 1969.

Berkley, G.   *The craft of public administration.* Boston: Allyn & Bacon, 1975.

Broom, L. & Selznick, P.   *Principles of sociology.* New York: Harper & Row, 1970.

Broomfield, M. T.   Conflict management: the Dayton, Ohio experience. In R. W. Kobetz (Ed.). *Crisis intervention and the police.* Gaithersburg, Maryland: International Association of Chiefs of Police, 1974.

Brown, L. P.   *Evaluation of police-community relations programs* (Doctoral dissertation, University of California, Berkeley, 1970). (University Microfilms No. 71-15,689).

Brown, L. P.   *The death of police community relations.* Occasional paper, Institute for Urban Affairs and Research, *I.* Washington, D.C.: Howard University, 1973.

Cambridge, Massachusetts Police Policy Manual. *Handling the mentally ill.* In R. W. Kobetz (Ed.). *Crisis intervention and the police.* Gaithersburg, Maryland: International Association of Chiefs of Police, 1974.

Campbell, A., & Schuman, H.   Attitudes of negroes towards the police. In P. Lerman (Ed.). *Delinquency and social policy.* New York: Praeger, 1970.

Caplan, H.   Quoted in W. Getz, A. E. Wiesen, S. Sue, & A. Ayers, *Fundamentals of crisis counseling.* Lexington, Mass.: Lexington Books, 1974.

Carkhuff, R. R. & Berenson, B. G.   *Beyond counseling and therapy.* New York: Holt, Rinehart & Winston, 1967.

Chwast, J.   Value conflicts in law enforcement. In A. Niederhoffer, & A.

Blumberg (Eds.). *The ambivalent force*. San Francisco: Rinehart Press, 1973.

Clifford, W., & Morris, N.   Participation of the public in the prevention and control of crime and delinquency. In J. T. Curran, A. Fowler, & R. H. Ward (Eds.). *Police and law enforcement 1972*. New York: AMS Press, 1973.

Cohn, Y.   Crisis intervention and the victim of robbery. In I. Dropkin (Ed.). *Victimology: a new focus*. Lexington, Mass.: Lexington Books, 1973.

Cromwell, P. F., & Keefer, G.   *Police-community relations*. St. Paul, Minn.: West, 1973.

Cumming, E., Cumming. I., & Edell, L.   Policeman as philosopher, guide and friend. *Social Problems*, 1965, *12*(3), 276-286.

Davis, J.   Law as a type of social control. In R. Akers, & R. Hawkins (Eds.). *Law and control in society*. Englewood Cliffs: Prentice-Hall, 1975.

Doig, J.   Police problems, proposals, and strategies for change. *Public Administration Review*, 1968, *28*(5), 393-403.

Engle, C. D.   Police training in non-crime related functions. *The Police Chief*, June, 1974, *41*, 61-66.

Finckenhauer, O. J.   *Police-community contacts and the stereotypic image of the police in a suburban community* (Doctoral dissertation, New York University, 1970). (University Microfilms No. 71-24,727).

Fink, J., & Sealy, L. G.   *The community and the police—conflict or co-operation?* New York: Wiley, 1974.

Fortier, K. N.   The Police culture—its effects on sound police-community relations. *The Police Chief*, February 1972, *39*, 33-35.

Furstenberg. F. F., & Welford, C. F.   Calling the police: the evaluation of police service. *Law and Society Review*, 1973, *7*(3), 393-406.

Galliher, J. F., Donavan, L. P., & Adams. D. L.   Small town police: trouble, tasks and public. *Journal of Police Science and Administration*, March 1975, *3*, 19-28.

Garbor, I. & Low, C.   The police role in the community. *Criminology*, 1973, *11*, 383-409.

Garmire, B. Understanding others; the police and the citizens. In A. F. Brandstatter, & L. Radelet (Eds.). *Police-community relations: a sourcebook*. Beverly Hills: The Glencoe Press, 1968.

Germann, A. C. Police planning and research as related to police-community relations. In A. F. Brandstatter, & L. Radelet (Eds.). *Police-community relations: a sourcebook*. Beverly Hills: The Glencoe Press, 1968.

Germann, A. C., Day, F., & Gallati, R. *Introduction to law enforcement and criminal justice*. Springfield, Ill.: Charles C. Thomas, 1962.

Goldstein, H. Police response to urban crisis. *Public Administration Review*, 1968, *28*, 417-423.

Gourley, D. D. The need for marketing in the police field. *The Police Chief*, July 1974, *41*, 16-18.

Grange, J. Understanding conflict: experience and behavior. *The Police Chief*, July 1974, *41*, 36-38.

Jacob, H. Black and white perceptions of justice in the city. *Law and Society Review*, 1971, *6*(1), 69-89.

Johnson, T. A. The application of organizational theory to the problems of police resistance to police community relations. *Journal of Police Science and Administration*, 1975, *3*(1), 84-94.

Katz, D., & Kahn, R. *The social psychology of organizations*. New York: Wiley, 1966.

Klyman, F. I. The police-community relations survey: a quantitative inventory of services and work units. *Journal of Police Science and Administration*, 1974, *2*(1), 77-81.

Korn, R., & McCorkle, L. *Criminology and penology*. New York: Holt, Rinehart & Winston, 1959.

Kowalewski, V. Police as helpers: new possibilities from the radical school. Paper presented at The First National Symposium on the Police and Humanities, American University, Washington, D.C., May 1974.

Kowalewski, V. Police and social services: breaking the barriers. *The Police Chief*, Sept. 1975, *42*, 259-262.

Kroes, W. H., Margolis, B. L., & Hurrell, J. J., Jr. Job stress in policemen. *Journal of Police Science and Administration*, 1974, 2(2), 145-155.

Lazarus, A. A. *Behavior therapy and beyond.* New York: McGraw Hill, 1971.

Lohman, J. D., & Misner, G. E. *The police and the community:* the dynamics of their relationship in a changing society. Vols. 1 & 2, Field Surveys IV, Washington, D.C.: U.S. Government Printing Office, 1967.

London, P. The end of ideology in behavior modification. *American Psychologist,* 1972, 27, 913-920.

Manning, P. The police: mandate, strategies, and appearances. In J. Douglas (Ed.). *Crime and justice in American society.* Indianapolis: Bobbs-Merrill, 1971.

McNamara, J. H. Uncertainties in police work: the relevance of police recruits' background and training. In D. J. Bordua (Ed.). *The police: six sociological essays.* New York: Wiley, 1967.

Miller, G. A. Psychology as a means of promoting human welfare. *American Psychologist,* 1969, 24, 1063-1075.

Mills, C. W. *The power elite.* London, Oxford University Press, 1956.

Motto, J. A., Brooks, R. M., Ross, C. P., & Allen, N. M. *Standards for suicide prevention and crisis centers.* New York: Behavioral Publications, 1974.

Munro, J. *Police organization and administrative behavior.* Cincinnati, Ohio: Anderson, 1974.

National Advisory Commission on Criminal Justice Standards and Goals: Task Force on Police. *Police.* Washington, D.C.: U.S. Government Printing Office, 1973.

Neubauer, D. W. *Criminal justice in middle America.* Morristown, N.J.: General Learning Press, 1974.

Niederhoffer, A. *Behind the shield.* New York: Doubleday, 1967.

Niederhoffer, A., & Blumberg A. S. *The ambivalent force: perspectives on the police.* San Francisco: The Rinehart Press, 1973.

Parad, H. J., & Resnik, H. L. P. The practice of crisis intervention in emergency care. In H. L. P. Resnik & H. L. Ruben (Eds.). *Emergency psychiatric care: the management of mental health crises.* Bowie, Maryland: The Charles Press, 1975.

Parker, L. C., & Meier, R. D. *Interpersonal psychology for law enforcement and corrections.* St. Paul: West, 1975.

President's Commission on Law Enforcement and the Administration of Justice. Washington, D.C.: U.S. Government Printing Office, 1967.

Purdy, E. The police as community leaders. *Police,* 1966, *10*(5).

Quinney, R. *Crime and justice in society.* Boston: Little Brown, 1969.

Quinney, R. *The social reality of crime.* Boston: Little Brown, 1970.

Radelet, L. Implications of professionalism in law enforcement for police-community relations. *Police,* 1966, *10*(6), 82-86.

Reese, C. D. Police training effects on racial prejudice. *Journal of Police Science and Administration,* 1973, *1*(3), 260-265.

Reiser, M. Policemen as mental health agents. In President's Commission on Law Enforcement and the Administration of Justice: Task Force Report: *The Police.* Washington, D.C.: U.S. Government Printing Office, 1967.

Reiser, M. *The police department psychologist.* Springfield, Illinois: Charles C. Thomas, 1972.

Reiser, M. Mental health in police work and training. *The Police Chief,* August 1974, *41*, 51-53.

Reiss, A. J. A civil police in a civil society. *Yale Reports,* 1969, *517*.

Reiss, A. J. *The police and the public.* New Haven: Yale University Press, 1971.

Report of the National Advisory Commission on Civil Disorders. New York: Bantam, 1968.

Resnik, H. L. P., & Ruben. H. E. (Eds.). *Emergency psychiatric care: the management of mental health crisis.* Bowie, Maryland: The Charles Press, 1975.

Riley, D. Should communities control their police? In J. T. Curran, A. Fowler, & R. H. Ward (Eds.). *Police and law enforcement 1972.* New York: AMS Press, 1973.

Rinzel, D. F. From a study in progress. Reported in H. W. More, Jr. *Critical Issues in Law Enforcement*. Cincinnati: Anderson, 1972.

San Diego Police Department. *Community profiling and police patrol* (Abstract). San Diego, California, December 1974.

Saunders, C. B. *Upgrading the American police*. Washington, D.C.: Brookings Institution, 1970.

Schur, E. M. *Our criminal society*. Englewood Cliffs: Prentice-Hall, 1969.

Schwartz, Fichtner, Bick and Associates. *Public safety: a master plan working paper*. Report to the City Plan Commission, New Britain, Connecticut, 1970.

Shneidman, E. Crisis intervention: some thoughts and perspectives. In G. A. Specter & W. L. Claiborn (Eds.). *Crisis intervention*. New York: Behavioral Publications, 1973.

Siegal, A., Federman, P. *Professional police—human relations training*. Springfield, Illinois: Charles C. Thomas, 1963.

Skolnick, J. *Justice without trial*. New York: Wiley, 1966.

Stark, R. *Police riots*. Belmont, California: Wadsworth Publishing Co., 1972.

Toch, H., Grant, J. D., & Galvin, R. T. *Agents of change: a study in police reform*. New York: Wiley, 1975.

Treger, H., Thomson, D., & Jaeck, G. S. A police social work model. *Crime and Delinquency*, 1974, *20*, 281-291.

Trojanowicz, R. C., & Dixon, S. L. *Criminal justice and the community*. Englewood Cliffs, N.J.: Prentice-Hall, 1974.

U.S. Department of Justice: The Federal Bureau of Investigation. *Uniform Crime Reports—1973*. Washington, D.C.: U.S. Government Printing Office, 1974.

Yinger, J. *Toward a field theory of behavior*. New York: McGraw-Hill, 1965.

Wambaugh, J. *The onion field*. New York: Dell, 1973.

Weber, Max. *Law and Economy in Society*, Max Rheinstein, Ed. Boston: Harvard University Press, 1954.

Westley, W. A.   *Violence and the police.* Cambridge, Mass.: MIT Press, 1970.

Whitehouse, J.   Historical perspectives on the police community service functions. *Journal of Police Science and Administration,* 1973, *1,* 87-92.

Wilson, J. Q.   Dilemmas of police administration. *Public Administration Review,* 1968, *28*(5), 407-417.

Wilson, J. Q.   *Varieties of police behavior.* Cambridge, Mass.: Harvard University Press, 1968.

Wilson, J. Q.   What makes a better policeman? *Atlantic Monthly,* 1969, *223,* 129-153.

Wilson, O. W.   *Police planning.* Springfield, Illinois: Thomas, 1952.

Zacker, J.   Is opposition to social intervention resistance or coping? *Professional Psychology,* 1974, 5, 198-205.

Zusman, J.   Recognition and management of psychiatric emergencies in emergency psychiatric care. In Resnik, H. L. P., & Ruben, H. L. (Eds.). *Emergency psychiatric care: the management of mental health crises.* Bowie, Maryland: The Charles Press, 1975.

Subject Index

T

Total role concept, 23

W

We-they dichotomy, 99, 139

U

Uniform crime report
  police deaths, 113
Unionization
  education and training, 99
United States Department of Justice
  victimization study, 150

Name Index